THE POCKET IDIOT'S GUIDE™ TO

Feng Shui

by Stephanie Roberts

ALPHA

A member of Penguin Group (USA) Inc.

ALPHA BOOKS

Published by the Penguin Group

Penguin Group (USA) Inc., 375 Hudson Street, New York, New York 10014, U.S.A.

Penguin Group (Canada), 10 Alcorn Avenue, Toronto, Ontario, Canada M4V 3B2 (a division of Pearson Penguin Canada Inc.)

Penguin Books Ltd, 80 Strand, London WC2R 0RL, England

Penguin Ireland, 25 St Stephen's Green, Dublin 2, Ireland (a division of Penguin Books Ltd)

Penguin Group (Australia), 250 Camberwell Road, Camberwell, Victoria 3124, Australia (a division of Pearson Australia Group Pty Ltd)

Penguin Books India Pvt Ltd, 11 Community Centre, Panchsheel Park, New Delhi—110 017, India

Penguin Group (NZ), cnr Airborne and Rosedale Roads, Albany, Auckland 1310, New Zealand (a division of Pearson New Zealand Ltd)

Penguin Books (South Africa) (Pty) Ltd, 24 Sturdee Avenue, Rosebank, Johannesburg 2196, South Africa

Penguin Books Ltd, Registered Offices: 80 Strand, London WC2R 0RL, England

Copyright © 2004 by Penguin Group (USA) Inc

THE POCKET IDIOT'S GUIDE TO and Design are trademarks of Penguin Group (USA) Inc.

International Standard Book Number: 1-59257-238-3
Library of Congress Catalog Card Number: 2004101846

08   8

Interpretation of the printing code: The rightmost number of the first series of numbers is the year of the book's printing; the rightmost number of the second series of numbers is the number of the book's printing. For example, a printing code of 04-1 shows that the first printing occurred in 2004.

Printed in the United States of America

Note: This publication contains the opinions and ideas of its author. It is intended to provide helpful and informative material on the subject matter covered. It is sold with the understanding that the author and publisher are not engaged in rendering professional services in the book. If the reader requires personal assistance or advice, a competent professional should be consulted.

The author and publisher specifically disclaim any responsibility for any liability, loss, or risk, personal or otherwise, which is incurred as a consequence, directly or indirectly, of the use and application of any of the contents of this book.

Most Alpha books are available at special quantity discounts for bulk purchases for sales promotions, premiums, fund-raising, or educational use. Special books, or book excerpts, can also be created to fit specific needs.

For details, write: Special Markets, Alpha Books, 375 Hudson Street, New York, NY 10014.

Contents

Introduction

Feng shui, sometimes called "the art of placement," is the ancient Chinese practice of arranging your home to create an auspicious and comfortable living environment. Today, feng shui is practiced on many different levels and in many different ways—some traditional, others contemporary—that range from extremely analytical to highly intuitive and encompass a wide variety of methods in between.

The goal of feng shui is always the same regardless of which methods you follow: to assist you in achieving success in all the important areas of your life. When your home has good feng shui, you are more likely to find happiness and fulfillment in romance, work, finances, family, creativity and so on—and to do so while living a healthy and balanced life.

What's Inside

The Pocket Idiot's Guide to Feng Shui provides practical ways to identify and correct potential feng shui problems and improve the energy and "flow" of your home. You won't find any complicated formulas or tables of numbers in this book. Here the focus is on how to look at your home and floor plan with feng shui eyes, identify necessary corrections, and choose simple changes to improve the energy of your home.

Here's what you'll find in this book.

Chapter 1 provides a brief overview of the ancient origins of feng shui, how the practice has evolved and expanded as it has been adopted by a modern Western audience, and why *you* are the most important ingredient in the feng shui of your home.

Chapter 2 focuses on the influence of landscape and setting of your home, including both natural and urban environmental factors.

Chapter 3 introduces two important tools that are used to both diagnose feng shui problems and correct or improve the energy of your home: the ba gua (a kind of feng shui energy map), and the five feng shui elements and how they support or control each other.

Chapter 4 shows you how to apply the ba gua to your home's floor plan and analyze which areas of your home are affecting what aspects of your life—and whether that influence is helping or hindering you.

Chapter 5 gives you suggestions for how to improve the flow of energy (chi) through your home by creating good feng shui around your front door, stairs, and hallways.

Chapter 6 addresses one of the big whammies of bad feng shui: clutter! By the time you've finished this chapter, you'll be motivated to roll up your sleeves and start clearing all that stuck energy out of your space.

Chapter 7 tells you all about secret arrows and other forms of sha chi (negative energy) that could be affecting your home and your family, as well as what you can do about them.

Chapters 8 through 13 take you on a room-by-room feng shui tour of your home, from kitchen to living and dining rooms, bedrooms, bathrooms, even your home office.

Chapter 14 gives you an insider's look at why good housekeeping is good feng shui, and why you shouldn't wait until it's time to sell your home to address its "curb appeal."

Two helpful appendixes are included as well. Appendix A provides a handy quick reference to the most common kinds of feng shui objects and where and how to use them. Appendix B directs you to helpful books and websites where you can get more information on both the traditional and modern practices of feng shui.

Featured Information

Throughout the text you will also find four different kinds of key information highlighted in boxes for your convenience:

Say "Chi"

Here you'll find definitions and explanations for key terms that should be part of your feng shui vocabulary.

Feng Fact

These boxes contain useful bits of background information that expand your understanding of feng shui.

It's Elemental

Check these boxes for helpful feng shui tips and hints that you can put into practice right away.

Sha Alert!

"Sha chi" is the feng shui name for harmful energy. The warnings in these boxes make sure you don't overlook any common feng shui problems.

Trademarks

All terms mentioned in this book that are known to be or are suspected of being trademarks or service marks have been appropriately capitalized. Alpha Books and Penguin Group (USA) Inc. cannot attest to the accuracy of this information. Use of a term in this book should not be regarded as affecting the validity of any trademark or service mark.

Ancient Roots, Modern Branches

In This Chapter

- The origins and purpose of feng shui
- How traditional practices have evolved to meet the needs of a contemporary western culture
- How the power of your intention supports the changes you make to your home

The ancient Chinese practice of feng shui (pronounced "fung shway"), widely used in Asia for thousands of years, is now increasingly popular in the West. Across the United States and around the world, thousands of people are discovering how simple changes in the selection, color, and arrangement of their furnishings can help improve the energy or chi of their homes and create supportive environments for fulfillment and success in all aspects of life.

Feng shui has evolved in significant ways as it has been embraced by a contemporary audience and adapted to twenty-first-century Western culture. While the traditional practices are still used—and are still effective today—there are now new ways to practice feng shui that do not require the use of a compass or complex calculations. (For those who are interested in exploring all forms of the art, *The Complete Idiot's Guide to Feng Shui, Second Edition* provides an excellent introduction to the traditional methods. See Appendix B for details.)

If you want to make a few simple changes to your home that will create a more comfortable, nurturing, and inspiring environment—without complicated charts or tables of numbers—this is the book for you. You'll learn how to increase the presence and movement of chi through your home so that it supports career success, financial prosperity, and romantic fulfillment. I'll help you recognize specific feng shui problems and teach you how to correct them with simple and appropriate changes for every room in your home.

What Is Feng Shui?

Feng shui is the art of creating living and working spaces that are comfortable, attractive, and harmonious with their environments. In its broadest sense, feng shui includes selection of a favorable site, design, and construction of the dwelling (or commercial building) in accordance with specific principles, and furnishing/decoration of the space to support prosperity, success, and happiness in all areas of life.

Most people today come to feng shui at the later stages of this process, after their home has been built and furnished. They use feng shui to identify potential ways in which the energy or *chi* of their space can be corrected or improved to encourage greater comfort, success, and good fortune. Their focus is on adjusting the décor and arrangement of their home.

Say "Chi"

Feng shui is often referred to as "acupuncture for the home," and with good reason. Part art and part science, feng shui involves analysis of the chi of a location or building, diagnosis of weaknesses or problems, and the selection and placement of appropriate cures and enhancements. **Chi** (sometimes spelled "qi") is the natural life force or energy that is present in all things. When we recognize that everything around us, ourselves included, is connected by the presence of this universal energy, we become aware that the chi of our space is an important aspect of our life experience.

The term feng shui combines the Chinese words for "wind" and "water," key factors in assessing the quality and movement of chi in a landscape.

The feng shui tips you will learn in this book help create a good quality and flow of chi in your home.

Dragon Veins and Flying Stars

In ancient China, feng shui was first used to locate auspicious settings for the tombs of emperors. It was thought that if the bones of revered ancestors were fortunately located, current and future generations would prosper.

Feng shui masters studied the shapes of mountain ridges and the curves of rivers to discern the underlying "dragon veins" within the land, which determined the flow of energy through a region. Certain configurations of hills, valleys, and rivers were thought to be auspicious, while others were considered unlucky. Over time, these principles came to be applied to selecting house sites for the living as well.

Once a site had been selected, elaborate charts of "Flying Stars" were examined to determine the best orientation for the structure. These "stars" are numbers that change regularly in a specific pattern based on the Chinese calendar. Some number combinations are good, others unlucky.

Today, the Flying Stars method is used both for new construction and to identify fortunate and unfortunate influences within an existing home. However, using this method requires getting an accurate compass reading, knowing the exact date of construction of the building (and of any major renovations), and determining the facing direction of the home—which is not necessarily the same as the front door. For urban apartment-dwellers, especially, these requirements are often impossible to meet.

Other traditional guidelines, such as that the kitchen should be located in the southern sector of the home, originated from the climate and geography of central China. This kind of advice does not necessarily translate well to other locations around the globe. In the hot, dry American Southwest, for example, the kitchen may be better placed on the cooler northern side of the home.

Another feng shui method widely practiced today uses an individual's gender and year of birth to define four lucky and four unlucky directions for each person. Choices of dwelling, room use, and furniture placement are made based on these superstitious orientations.

Unfortunately, many people who attempt to follow these guidelines without using them in the appropriate context end up creating more feng shui problems than they solve. For example, it will do little good to place your bed so that you sleep with your head in a "lucky" direction if it means the bed itself is poorly located in the room or that while you sleep you will be exposed to "sha chi" (negative energy) from that position.

The traditional and contemporary methods of feng shui provide different paths to the same end. Just as acupuncture, shiatsu, and Western forms of massage all act to clear and balance the energy in the physical body, the purpose of both traditional and contemporary feng shui is to adjust and balance the energy in your home.

 Feng Fact _____

> Strict traditionalists may argue that theirs is the only true feng shui, but this attitude fails to acknowledge that the ancient practices have significant drawbacks for many contemporary users. The modern forms of feng shui evolved specifically to provide solutions and alternatives that address these issues.

Feng Shui Heads West

The traditional forms of feng shui are based on the seasonal and magnetic influences of the earth. Today, especially in an urban environment, these natural influences are often distorted by the closer or more powerful effects of nearby power lines and the appliances that fill our homes.

Steel structural beams, underground power or subway lines, cars parked along the street in front of your house, the refrigerator in your kitchen, and even the computer on your desk can all have a significant impact on the electro-magnetic fields in your environment.

If you want to practice the traditional Flying Stars method of feng shui, you may find that you get different compass readings at different places around your home and that it's impossible to determine which one is correct. Since even a couple of degrees can make a difference to the Flying Stars configuration, you may be unable to determine which chart applies to your home.

If you don't know when your home was built, you can't use this method at all. And good luck figuring out what to do if you live in the southern hemisphere! Traditional practitioners are unable to agree on whether to follow the classical arrangement of the stars or flip everything around backward when you're "down under."

Contemporary feng shui adapts the ancient principles of auspicious and inauspicious landscape forms to both exterior and interior spaces. Inventing effective ways to use the basic tools of the art without consulting the compass makes feng shui available to anyone, anywhere.

Another drawback to traditional feng shui is that it defines specific "bad" situations with the assumption that we will then avoid them. Often it doesn't provide much in the way of constructive advice about what to do if the place that we are living in exhibits those problems.

In the Western Hemisphere, most of us learn about feng shui after we have settled in the place where we now live, when it's too late to use the traditional feng shui guidelines for selecting a home. And when we are in the market for a new place to live, our main concerns are to find a home that we can afford, of an appropriate size and configuration for our family, and in a neighborhood that offers the amenities we need. Real estate values, community safety, convenience to schools, stores, recreation, and the length of our commute to work are all important factors in our housing decisions. Job transitions, school calendars, and eager buyers for our old home often result in a hurried move.

Finding a home that meets all of our other requirements is often difficult enough, and whether or not we can find a place with good feng shui may be the last thing we think about. Far more frequently, we make our housing decisions based on practical considerations and worry about feng shui after we move in.

 Feng Fact

> Compared to the traditional practices, contemporary feng shui places much greater emphasis on what you can do to correct and improve a less-than-ideal situation. It acknowledges the impact of your personal energy and style on your space, and encourages a highly personalized selection of enhancements and cures. It prompts you to use your own good sense and intuition, rather than relying on one-size-fits-all rules.

The modern practice of feng shui, while deeply rooted in the traditional teachings, focuses on creating a nourishing flow of energy (chi) through your space, and on removing or correcting negative influences. While money, romance, and health are perennial top issues, many of us are also seeking feng shui help for modern concerns such as depression, stress, self-esteem, and uncertainty about our life direction, all of which can be addressed by the contemporary practice.

The Power of Your Intention

Many people think the results they hope to get from feng shui will come just from the crystals and wind chimes they've hung around the house, the romantic imagery placed in the bedroom, or the prosperity cures in the living room. What they may not realize is that their own intention is a powerful tool for creating positive change. Feng shui works best when it is directed toward clear personal objectives and enlivened by detailed visualization of the desired end result.

Visualizing Success

For each area of life that you would like to improve—such as increasing your income, attracting a new romantic partner, or finding a better job—imagine how achieving your goals will change your daily experiences. Want money for a new sports car? Imagine the smell of the leather upholstery, the pristine gleam of the finish, and the sound of the engine as you accelerate. Need a new job? Imagine answering your phone and hearing your new employer say "You got the job. How soon can you start?" See yourself setting up your new work space and handling your new responsibilities with ease.

Make your visualizations as specific, concrete, and detailed as you can. Imagine place, time of day, what you are wearing, even the weather. The more senses you involve and the more excitement you can feel, the more powerful your visualization will be.

As you make the feng shui changes that are designed to support and encourage the achievement of your goals, take a few minutes each day to play out these imagined scenarios in your mind. Remember to imagine the outcome not as something that you desire to receive in the future, but as something that has already manifested for you.

When you can feel the joy and satisfaction of experiencing your dreams coming true, you know that you are applying your intention effectively, and that your visualization is working powerfully on an energetic level to support your feng shui changes.

No Need to Feel Overwhelmed

Many people, when they first learn about feng shui, rush around hanging wind chimes and crystals in their Wealth or Relationship areas (you'll learn where there are in Chapters 3 and 4) without pausing to take a systematic look at their entire home to identify the areas or problems that should be addressed first.

Sometimes the most powerful change can be accomplished by one very minor adjustment. If you are making a lot of other changes at the same time, the impact of the critical adjustment might actually be minimized by all the other shifts going on.

Sha Alert!

The classic advice, "If it ain't broke, don't fix it," is often overlooked in feng shui. Making lots of unnecessary feng shui changes all at once can create chaotic energy in the home, and may even trigger undesired shifts in situations that you were happy with the way they were.

Feng shui works best when you focus on one key area at a time, and prioritize your changes so that the most pressing problems are addressed before you indulge in fun but nonessential improvements.

The Least You Need to Know

- The practice of feng shui today includes many different forms and methods, some ancient, some contemporary.
- Modern feng shui techniques do not require a compass or complicated calculations.
- Feng shui can be adapted to any style of décor.
- Your clear and focused attention on achieving the outcomes you desire is the most powerful feng shui tool available to you.

Natural and Manmade Landscapes

In This Chapter

- Features of the ideal feng shui location
- The role of mountains and rivers in feng shui
- How the slope of your land could be affecting your home
- How the traffic on your street influences your luck

Good feng shui begins with the setting and landscape surrounding your home. When the chi of your neighborhood is strong, and your home is in a good location, your luck and prosperity will be supported. If you live in an area where the chi is weak, or in a home that is not well situated, feng shui enhancements and corrections—both inside and outside the home—will be even more important.

Buildings Are Mountains

The ideal feng shui location is described as being like a comfortable armchair, with a mountain or large hill behind the house and two smaller hills on either side. The front of the property is open, and slopes gently down to a body of water such as a lake or river. In many communities, the wealthier neighborhoods are in just such locations: up in the hills above town, where prosperous residents can enjoy the best views, coolest breezes, and freshest air. Wherever you live, if your home enjoys fresh air and a pleasant view, it's got a lot of positive energy.

The "armchair location" provides support at the back and protection on the sides, while leaving the front open.

These important functions of support and protection can also be provided by other features, such as trees, a stone wall, fence, or large boulders. In a very flat landscape, even a slight rise in the land can function as a mountain.

In an urban setting, the buildings around you are the "mountains" that form the armchair. A good feng shui setting in the city has a taller building behind, somewhat lower buildings to either side, and an open view to the front, such as is provided by the plaza in front of an office building, the small garden or yard in front of a townhouse, or the entry courtyard of an apartment complex.

Suburban settings often combine both rural and urban features. The "armchair" for your home might be created by the slope of a hill behind the house, a neighbor's home on one side, and some large trees and a stone wall along the edge of your property on the other side. Your front yard is the open area to the front.

Balance and Proportion

In feng shui, balance and proportion are always important. The hills, buildings, or other features that form the back and arms of your home's "armchair" should be large enough to feel supporting and protective, like a parent or older sibling walking beside a child, but not so large that they dominate the house.

A very large, steep hill can be more threatening than protective; it may even create a risk of mudslides or rocks falling on your home. A neighboring building that is of a much larger scale—such as a high-rise apartment building next door to a single-family home—can be oppressive in a similar way. If this is true for your home, lights that shine up at the house from ground level, and flags or banners on the roof or around the house will strengthen and lift the chi.

If you live in an apartment building that is over-shadowed by much larger neighbors, bright paint colors and good lighting will help keep the chi of your home strong. Dark paint, dark wood, low lights and lots of heavy furniture will all increase the oppressive energy, rather than counteracting it.

When the back or arms of the armchair are significantly smaller in scale, or are missing completely, your location may feel vulnerable and exposed. Landscaping elements can be chosen to create a virtual armchair: erect a strong fence, plant trees, or create a small hill to the back with a few truck-loads of rocks and topsoil. Even the simple addition of a large stone or piece of garden statuary can make a difference.

Chi Rolls Downhill

The ideal armchair location has a gentle slope to the front of the property. Where the land slopes gently away from the house, you have a good view from your slightly higher elevation. In a flat location, your view to the front may not be as extensive, but chi will be able to circulate easily around your property. A hill that is too steep is more of a problem, because chi always tends to roll downhill.

If your home is high above the street, it will be difficult for chi to reach your house. Given this, you might think that a home below street level on the downhill side of the street would be a better choice, because chi will flow easily down toward you. This is true; the drawback is that it will be harder for you to get back uphill and out into the world. You may find that you stay at home a lot, that your social life suffers because you just don't feel like going out, or that you lack initiative for pursuing new projects. For someone who works at home, this might not be a problem. If you are in a sales or other profession that requires a lot of customer contact and networking, that slope could be working against you.

It's Elemental

Install a bright light or wind chime at the top of a steep driveway to help lift the chi uphill. Where a house is high above the street, place the light or wind chime near the house. If the house is below street level, place the light or wind chime at the street end of the path or driveway.

In a city setting, the sunken entrance to a basement apartment or the high stoop of a brownstone townhouse create similar problems. Again, the cure is to lift and attract chi to the higher side of the steps or path. In addition to lights and wind chimes, flags, banners, bright signage and illuminated signs or house numbers can help create the desired effect.

Reversed Positions

Where the yard slopes downhill at the back of the house, it's as though the house is sitting backward in its armchair. The front of the house faces the back of the chair, and the back of the house is open and unprotected. That's trouble enough in feng shui terms, and this difficult position is made even worse because chi can roll downhill right out the backyard, taking your luck, energy, and financial resources with it.

It is important to understand that a front door or main entry on the uphill side of the house does not necessarily mean you have this problem. The key is to identify the *facing direction* of your house.

Say "Chi"

The side of your home that has the most windows, the best light, the best view, and the most activity is the **facing direction**. This might not be the same side of the house where the street and/or your front door are located.

Remember the armchair analogy: Your home should be seated in the armchair of the surrounding landscape so that it looks out the open side. A sloping yard is not a problem if the downhill slope is on the facing side of the house, regardless of the location of the front door or main entry. If the facing side of the house is toward the back of the armchair, however, this is a reversed and inauspicious position.

In a typical suburban residential neighborhood, both the facing direction and the front door are usually on the street side of the home. Here, a backyard that slopes downhill away from the house is a potential feng shui challenge. The steeper the slope, the bigger the problem.

The solution is to contain the chi at the back of your property in some way, such as with a solid fence or wall. A swimming pool at the back of the house may also help, as the contained water of the pool will collect and contain chi; however, the pool needs to be as close as possible to the rear property line for this to be an effective solution. If there are lots of trees at the back of the property, hanging a large wind chime in the lowest corner will help to lift the energy there. If you don't have any trees there, consider planting some; they will help to both contain and lift chi so it doesn't leak away as quickly.

Speaking of slopes, if the land beneath your home is so steep that part of your house is supported on pilings, your "armchair" doesn't have any seat. Regardless of how strong and sturdy those posts are, your home is energetically unsupported.

Although there's not much you can do to cure a setting like this, stones placed at all the outside corners of the house can symbolically ground and stabilize the structure. Of course, you're also well advised to keep your homeowner's insurance up to date, get a structural engineer to check your foundation, and hope your neighborhood isn't hit with a flood, mudslide, or earthquake.

Sha Alert!

Any location where your home is at risk from potential landslides, falling rocks, floods, or other natural disasters does not have good feng shui. A gorgeous view, beautiful landscaping, great architecture, and attractive furnishings cannot entirely overcome the negative chi of an unstable location.

Roads Are Rivers

In the preceding section we looked at how mountains—including the virtual mountains of surrounding hills, buildings, and landscaping— can create an armchair-like setting for your home. There's another important aspect of this auspicious configuration, and that is the presence of water— preferably the moving water of a stream or river—in front of the house, at the open side of the armchair.

Any view of water, such as a lake, ocean, or river, from the front of your house is good feng shui. Next best is a pond, stream, or swimming pool somewhere on your property. You can even attract the auspicious chi of moving water to your home by installing a fountain near the front door.

Just as buildings function as virtual mountains, roads are virtual rivers carrying people, commerce, and chi toward and away from your home.

Feng Fact _____

In pre-industrial times, rivers were the primary carriers of commerce and people. Virtually all the urban centers of the ancient world were located on rivers and at river deltas. The best agricultural areas were also located along rivers; without water, crops cannot grow. This concentration of human and commercial chi around rivers is the origin of the feng shui association of moving water with prosperity.

Speed and Direction

Balance and proportion are important for the "rivers" near your home, just as they are for "mountains." The ideal road is gently curving and not too heavily traveled, with traffic that moves at an appropriate speed for the neighborhood. The direction and speed of traffic around your home is a good indication of the direction and flow of chi.

A well-designed subdivision is likely to have good feng shui streets, with meandering curves that keep chi moving and speed bumps to prevent both traffic and chi from picking up too much speed.

A major road or high-speed highway near your home can create too much fast-moving chi for comfort. Depending on your home's location relative to the highway, it could either be sending too much chi your way, or rushing past so quickly that the chi is pulled away from your house. If the chi around your property is moving too fast, you can help stabilize and hold it with large rock or boulders in the yard. A swimming pool or pond also helps to collect and contain chi; even a birdbath or small water garden can be effective.

Houses that face a "T" intersection should be protected from the flow of chi coming down the street at them. We think of chi as a good thing, but when it moves too quickly it can be harmful. When a street—or even an alley—points directly at a building, the residents will be subject to increased stress and unsettled energy. This can be good for a business location, as it helps brings in customers, but for a residence it indicates a high probability of both health and financial problems.

The feng shui solution for a T-intersection or any other form of "sha chi" (negative energy) aimed at the house, is a specific cure called a ba gua (sometimes spelled "bagua," "pakua," or "pa kua") mirror. This is a small round mirror in an eight-sided frame decorated with specific combinations of solid and broken lines in sets of three. Mirrors reflect things, so when aimed at a source of sha chi—such as fast-moving traffic coming toward your house— they bounce that negative energy back the way it came.

The correct way to hang a ba gua mirror is with the three unbroken lines (which represent heaven) at the top and the three broken lines (which represent Earth) at the bottom.

You can find ba gua mirrors in a variety of sizes at most feng shui retailers (see Appendix B) and Asian products stores. If you don't have a ba gua mirror (or don't want to use one for aesthetic reasons), any small mirror or other highly reflective surface can be used in the same way.

A ba gua mirror protects this home against sha chi from the "T" intersection

A ba gua mirror is a powerful antidote to sha chi outside the home, but it should never be used indoors.

Dead Ends and Cul-de-Sacs

Dead-end streets and cul-de-sacs create some feng shui challenges for the people living along them. A through street enables a steady flow of traffic in and out of the area in both directions. On dead-end streets and cul-de-sacs, traffic comes on from one direction, stops or slows, turns around, then goes back out the way it came in.

Sha Alert!

A ba gua mirror is an exterior cure used to reflect sha chi away from a building and its occupants. Don't use this kind of mirror inside your home; its powerful effect is too strong for interior spaces, and it is said to cause bad luck if used indoors.

Because these streets have no through traffic, the flow of chi is lower than on the other streets of the neighborhood, which puts the residents of these blocks at an energetic disadvantage. On the plus side, these locations do tend to be quieter (lots of chi can mean lots of noise!), which in our hectic, high-stress world makes them desirable.

It's important to be aware, however, that a lack of noise and traffic does signal a lack of chi, so if you want more and better opportunities to come knocking at your door, a more active social life, or greater cash flow, you may want to attract chi to your door with:

- A wind chime by the front door
- A flagpole or banner in your yard
- A water fountain in the yard, preferably close to the front door

In a cul-de-sac, the chi that came down the street moves around the circle and flows right back out again without stopping. Here, it's a good idea to supplement the cures to attract chi to your door with some kind of large, heavy object—such as a decorative boulder or garden statue, or even a birdbath—near the sidewalk or road to help weigh chi down and keep it on your property.

The Least You Need to Know

- A good feng shui location is protected at the back and sides, and open at the front.
- The buildings neighboring your home can provide support and protection, or they might overshadow or block your property.
- Moving water at the front of the house increases luck and prosperity.
- Traffic on the roads around your home indicates the flow of chi toward, through, or past your property.

Chapter 3

Keys to Transformation

In This Chapter

- Understanding the ba gua energy map
- The qualities of the five feng shui elements
- How to incorporate the five elements into your decor

The practice of feng shui involves analyzing the chi of your home, diagnosing problems, identifying opportunities for improvement, and choosing the cures and enhancements that will be most helpful for you. This chapter introduces two basic tools that you will use to decide what solutions are right for your home: the ba gua and the five elements.

The Eight Areas of Influence

Knowing which areas of your space affect what aspects of your life enables you to make informed decisions about where to focus your feng shui attention and how to prioritize potential changes and enhancements.

The *ba gua*, which is a kind of energy map, can be used for any kind of space. The exterior mirror cure discussed in Chapter 2 is called a "ba gua" mirror because its design reflects the eight areas of this universal energy map. There is a ba gua for your entire property, a ba gua for your house or apartment, and a ba gua for each room in your home, and so on. You can even apply the ba gua to a piece of furniture, such as your bed, desk, or stove. (I'll show you exactly how to apply the ba gua map to your home in Chapter 4.)

Say "Chi"

The **ba gua** (meaning "eight areas") is a map of the energy in a space. It identifies how the chi in various areas in and around your home affects specific aspects of your life experience.

The ba gua divides any space into eight sections surrounding a central area called the Tai Chi. The Tai Chi connects all the other areas, so anything that affects the Tai Chi will impact every other aspect of your life as well.

This diagram shows the primary meanings of each area of the ba gua, including the eight outer areas and the central Tai Chi.

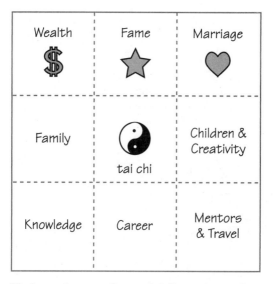

Wealth $	Fame ☆	Marriage ♡
Family	☯ tai chi	Children & Creativity
Knowledge	Career	Mentors & Travel

The ba gua is a map of energetic influences in your home.

There are other layers of meaning which may be useful in understanding what impact feng shui problems or challenges may have on your home, based on their location:

- The *Career* area concerns your life path and social connections as well as your work.

- The *Knowledge* area has to do with formal education as well as spirituality and self-awareness.

- The *Family* area includes your relatives as well as close friends you welcome into your family; it also has to do with your community and your ability to initiate new projects.

- The *Wealth* area is about "fortunate blessings" in any form, not just financial; your ability to receive is reflected here.

- The *Fame* area has to do with your reputation and how others perceive you; it is also about self-perception, your vision of the future, and inspiration in any form.

- The *Marriage* area includes romantic relationships of all kinds, business partnerships, mothers and mother figures, and your ability to care for yourself and receive nurturing from others.

- The *Children & Creativity* area has to do with the things and ideas that you bring into the world; it also affects your ability to complete what you started and to enjoy the fruits of your efforts.

- The *Mentors & Travel* area includes the assistance you receive from others, as well as the support that you provide, and your relationship with your father and other male authority figures.

- The *Tai Chi* area relates to your overall health and life balance; whatever happens here affects all the other areas as well.

When you are aware of the many different meanings of each area, or gua, you gain greater insight into the potential ways that feng shui problems could be affecting you.

> **It's Elemental** _____
>
> The K.I.S.S. factor ("Keep It Simple, Sweetie") is a good guideline for feng shui. Usually the most obvious meaning or connection is the right one.

For example, sha chi (negative energy) in the Mentors & Travel area could show up as disagreements and conflict with your manager. Because this appears as a work issue your first thought might be to look at your Career area. Recognizing that this is really about "support" from a "male authority figure"—which are Mentor issues—helps you fine-tune your feng shui focus, corrections and changes.

The Five Transformations

The five Chinese elements—wood, fire, earth, metal, and water—define five different qualities of chi. They are sometimes called the five "transformations," because each element defines a specific kind of energy and movement that can transform or change the chi of a space. Each element is associated with specific colors, shapes, and types of objects:

- Wood: upward, growing energy; all shades of green; columns and tall shapes, vertical stripes; any kind of plant or tree

- Fire: expansive, excited energy; reds and oranges; triangular, pointed, and jaggedly irregular shapes; flames (such as candles or a fireplace), lights, and electricity

- Earth: settling, stable, containing energy; browns and beiges; flat, square shapes; stones and smooth crystals, brick and ceramic objects, vases and containers

- Metal: contracting, introverted energy; white, gray, and metallic colors (silver, gold, copper, bronze); round and oval shapes; coins, metal objects, pointed crystals

- Water: flowing energy; blacks and blues; meandering and smoothly irregular shapes; liquids of all kinds, mirrors

By adjusting the balance of the elements in a space using the materials, shapes, and colors listed above, you can adjust the quality of the energy in that space. Adding more fire energy (such as a grouping of red candles, or decorating with red paint, fabric, or accent pieces) can help you feel more energized, while earth energy (such as ceramic accent pieces, for example) is stabilizing and helps you feel grounded and secure. Water energy (either in the form of real water or water imagery and colors) enhances intuition and communication, while metal (in the form of metallic materials, shapes, or colors) helps you tune out distractions and focus on details. Wood energy (plants, flowers, and all shades of green) supports steady progress on your work and helps you get new projects off the ground.

The Elements and the Ba Gua

Each area of the ba gua is associated with a specific element as well as specific colors:

- Career: water; black and dark blues
- Knowledge: earth; browns and light blues
- Family: young wood; medium and light greens
- Wealth: mature wood; dark greens and purple
- Fame: fire; reds and bright oranges
- Marriage: earth; pinks, reds, pastel earth tones
- Children & Creativity: smooth metal; white and metallic
- Mentors & Travel: sharp metal; gray, white, and metallic
- Tai Chi: earth; yellow

As you choose feng shui objects and cures to place in your home, keep the element associations in mind and choose objects that support or control the energy of the space depending on what effect you desire.

Decorating with the Elements

The furnishings and décor in each room of your home should include all of the five elements, but they do not need to be equally represented. One or two of the elements should set the tone for the room, with the others used as accents. What energies are dominant in your home décor right now? How does that shift from room to room?

> **It's Elemental** _____
>
> A small collection of objects and colors representing each of the five elements helps to balance the energy of a space.

Many objects have a combination of several different energies. For example, a round red box has a metal shape and a fire color; as a container it also has earth energy. A tall white candle embossed with a vine pattern is a fire object with a wood shape and pattern, in a metal color. Mixed-energy objects such as these are useful for ensuring that every element is represented in each space. To the round red box, you could add a smooth black river stone (water) wrapped in a piece of green fabric (wood), to complete the representation of all five elements. The white candle (fire, wood, metal) could be placed on a ceramic plate (earth) with a dark blue (water) glaze to create a combination of all five elements.

The best place for a five-element collection such as this is in the center of the room if the arrangement of your furniture allows: as a dining table centerpiece, for example, or on the living room coffee table. Other good spots, if the center won't work, include a fireplace mantle, a bedside or foyer table, an office bookcase, or the corner of your kitchen counter.

Friend or Foe?

In order to use colors, shapes, and materials to adjust the chi in different areas of your home, you need to understand how the different types of energy interact with each other:

- Wood feeds fire, disturbs earth, dulls metal, and absorbs water
- Fire creates earth (think of a volcano), melts metal, evaporates water, and burns wood
- Earth births metal, blocks water, impedes wood, and exhausts fire
- Metal creates water (like condensation on a cold can of soda on a hot day), chops wood, weakens fire, and depletes earth
- Water nourishes wood, extinguishes fire, washes away earth, and depletes metal

These relationships are summarized in the following diagrams.

In the first diagram we see that each element creates the next in a clockwise direction, shown by the dark curved arrows. Creating takes work; it reduces the strength of the creating element, the same way a long day at work leaves you feeling tired and hungry. In the second diagram, the reducing cycle is shown by the faded broken arrows.

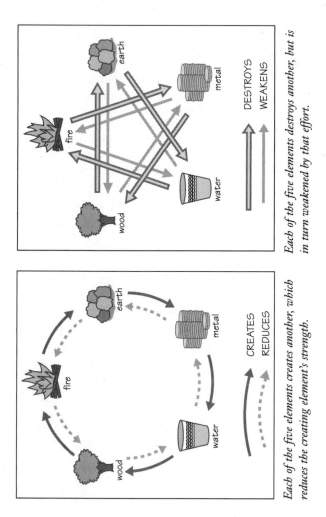

Each of the five elements destroys another, but is in turn weakened by that effort.

Each of the five elements creates another, which reduces the creating element's strength.

In the second diagram, we see how each element destroys or controls another, shown by the hollow arrows. Destruction is hard work, too, and it weakens the destroying element, as shown by the narrow straight arrows. For example, metal destroys wood, but chopping a lot of wood dulls an axe blade. And water puts out fire, but some of that water will be turned to steam in the process.

These interactions among the elements are a lot to absorb at first, but once you learn the creative and destructive patterns, it becomes quite easy.

Keep in mind that your first point of reference is the ba gua energy map. If you are struggling with money issues, for example, and hope that feng shui will help improve your finances, the first thing to do is find where the Wealth area is in your home (you'll learn how to do this in Chapter 4). Then, find the Wealth areas of the major rooms in your home, such as the living room, kitchen, and your bedroom. The Wealth area of a room that is in the Wealth area of house will be a good place for feng shui enhancements.

Based on the information in this chapter, you know that good colors for the Wealth area are dark greens and purples, and that the element associated with this area is wood. An easy way to enhance each of your wealth areas, then, is to add living or life-like plants—or pictures of plants and trees—and to use lots of green and purple colors in your furnishings and artwork.

Next, consult the element diagrams for additional ideas. Coins are a pretty obvious symbol of money, so you might think of adding some coins to your Wealth area. But—uh oh!—you realize that coins are metal, which destroys the wood energy associated with Wealth.

Looking at the element diagrams, you see that adding something to represent water will reduce the metal energy and, at the same time, strengthen wood. You decide to put nine Chinese coins in a black lacquer bowl and set it in the Wealth area of your living room on top of a piece of purple fabric.

Admiring your new feng shui enhancement, you notice a photograph of a Southwestern sunset on the wall beside your bowl. "Hmmm," you ponder, "that picture has lots of red and yellow colors in it; that means it has fire and earth energy, which will weaken wood. Maybe I should put that somewhere else instead."

Now you're getting the hang of it!

The Least You Need to Know

- The ba gua energy map shows you which areas of your home are affecting what aspects of your life.
- Include a little bit of each of the five elements in every space.
- Choose feng shui cures and enhancements based on the element energies appropriate to the ba gua area you are working on.

A New Look at Your Floor Plan

In This Chapter

- How to use the ba gua energy map
- Analyzing your feng shui floor plan
- What to do about "missing areas" and irregular house shapes

In Chapter 3 you learned about the ba gua—the feng shui map of the energetic influences in your space. Now it's time to take a look at how that map applies to the specific layout of your home, and see what it reveals about potential feng shui strengths and challenges.

The Compass or the Doorway?

One of the biggest sources of confusion in feng shui today is figuring out how the ba gua map applies to your specific home or office.

Traditionalists associate each gua with a specific compass direction:

- Career = North
- Fame = South
- Family = East
- Children & Creativity = West
- Knowledge = Northeast
- Mentors & Travel = Northwest
- Wealth = Southeast
- Marriage = Southwest

Feng Fact

The Career area is shown in the center of the bottom row of the ba gua because this area of the ba gua is associated with the direction North, and Chinese convention shows North at the bottom and South at the top. This is exactly the reverse of the Western practice of showing North at the top and South at the bottom. It makes sense, though, when you think of North as representing cold, dark, heavy, slow energy, and South as representing hot, bright, light, active energy. Since heat rises and cold sinks, the Chinese method makes perfect sense.

Many people still use this method and you can, too, if you want to. The disadvantage is that there is no consistency from room to room in where the various areas of influence are located relative to the layout of the space. The Wealth area might be in the front of one room, and at the back of another. Don't try to use guesswork for this method; you must use a compass to get accurate directional readings.

Modern feng shui recognizes that our relationship to a space is most strongly influenced by how we move through it. The contemporary Western practice is to orient the ba gua so that the lower edge (with the Career area in the center) lines up with the wall where the entry to the space is located.

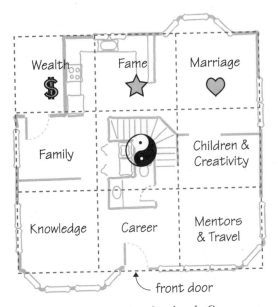

The modern ba gua is oriented so that the Career area is in the center of the front of the house or other space.

You can see that we can enter through the Knowledge, Career, or Mentors & Travel areas, depending on whether the door is in the center of the wall (as in the example shown in the diagram) or off to one side or the other. With this method, the Fame area is always in the center of the space on the far side. Wealth is always in the far left corner, and the Marriage area is always to the far right.

This modern use of the ba gua acknowledges the psychology of our relationship to our external environment; as we move into a space, what lies ahead of us (the Fame area) is associated with future vision, and what lies behind us (the Career area) represents the life path that has brought us to the present moment.

 It's Elemental

> The ba gua applies to your entire property, too. Just align the lower edge of the ba gua with the side of your yard that borders the street. The beginning of your driveway is the "entry" to your property.

Keep in mind that, with the doorway method, the dividing lines in a diagram show a much sharper boundary between the ba gua areas than really exists. Each gua occupies roughly one third of the length and width of the home or room. The guas blend into each other rather than changing abruptly from one to the next. As you identify how the ba gua fits over your floor plan, use the natural

division of nearby walls and hallways to identify
which rooms are in which areas. There is no need
to use a tape measure to find the exact point where
one gua ends and the other begins.

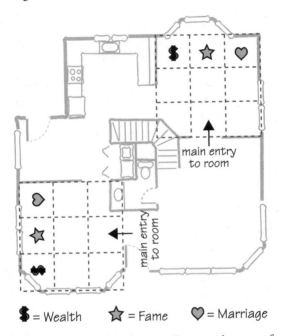

$ = Wealth   ☆ = Fame   ♡ = Marriage

*The ba gua for each room also places Career at the center of
the side of the room through which you enter the space. This
may mean rotating the ba gua one way or the other compared
to the ba gua for the entire house.*

In a multi-story house, each floor will have its own
ba gua. The "entry" to a floor above (or below) the
main level is at the top (or bottom) of the staircase
that provides access to that level. It is often difficult

to figure out how the ba gua should go in these cases, so it's okay to just look at the ba guas for the individual rooms on that level.

Do you have a sense now of where the main areas of influence in your home are? Based on what your key life issues are at this time, think about which sections of the ba gua are most relevant to you. Then look to see where those areas are in your home, as well as in each of the main rooms in your home: the kitchen, living room, home office (if you've got one), and your bedroom. These will be key places for feng shui cures and enhancements.

House Shapes and the Ba Gua

If you don't have a floor plan of your home available, take a moment now to draw one. Include the front door and the door or entry to each major room. It's okay to keep your diagram simple, as long as you take time to measure accurately and use a consistent scale so that the final result is also accurate.

If you live in a home that is a neat, rectangular shape, applying the ba gua to your space will be easy. Just line up the Career side of the ba gua with the side of the house that the front door is in, and stretch the grid to the back and side walls so it covers the entire structure.

An attached garage that shares a roof with the house is included in the ba gua, as are enclosed year-round areas such as a sunroom. Do not include screened or open porches or patios in the ba gua. Remember that the ba gua is always aligned with the door that the architect designed as the main entry to your home, even if you usually go in and out another way.

Applying the ba gua to a house with an irregular outline can be a little tricky. It helps to imagine that the ba gua is a huge blanket that you are laying over your home so that front edge of the blanket is lined up with the front door, and the other edges line up with the side and back walls of the house or apartment as closely as possible.

Parts of the house that stick out from under the blanket are called extensions. Places where the blanket/ ba gua stretches over space outside the house are missing areas.

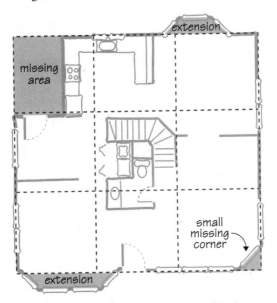

Extensions stick out from the main outline of the house; indentations are missing areas.

If you aren't sure whether you've got an extension or a missing area, compare the width of the part that sticks out to the width of the open area beside it. The smaller one is the extension or missing area:

- If the part that sticks out is wider (more than half the total width of that side of the house), it is covered by the ba gua and has a missing area next to it.

- If it is less than half the total width, it is an extension, and is not included in the ba gua.

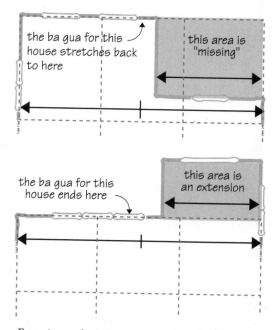

Extensions and missing areas are always less than half the width of that side of the house.

Extensions expand the energy of the gua they extend from, and are often a good place for feng shui enhancements. Generally, extensions are considered positive features for the house, but sometimes part of the house (often the garage) extends forward of the front door. This is often a sign that the activities associated with those rooms tend to take place away from home.

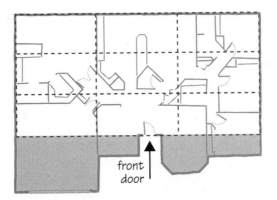

front
door

These shaded areas are all extensions
because they extend forward of
a recessed front door

Areas of the home that extend in forward of a recessed front door can symbolically push the activities associated with that space out of the house.

A family room in front of the door, for example, could mean that your leisure activities tend to mostly happen outside the home. A garage in this position (very common) can mean you are away from home a lot. A master bedroom forward of the door may indicate that someone isn't spending as much time at home as he or she should, perhaps for illicit reasons.

The cure for this situation, if you think you need one, is to hang a large mirror on the back wall of the room. This pulls the energy of that space back into the main body of the house.

What to Do About Missing Areas

Missing areas indicate a weakness in the energy of that area of the home. For example, if you live in a home that is missing the Wealth corner, it may be difficult for you to prosper there; even if you make a lot of money you may suffer from unexpected losses, or your expenses may continue to rise along with your income.

Sha Alert!

A missing Marriage area can make it difficult for a single person to find a partner; for a couple it may indicate dissatisfaction with the relationship.

Even a small missing area in a gua that corresponds to a difficult aspect of your life deserves priority attention. A missing area can be cured by energetically completing the outline of that space as shown in the following diagram. The placement of these remedies must be very accurate in order for this method to work.

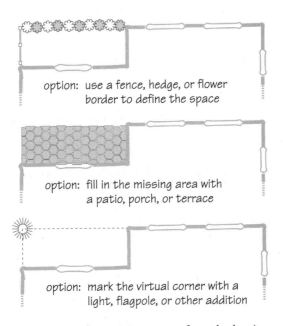

option: use a fence, hedge, or flower
border to define the space

option: fill in the missing area with
a patio, porch, or terrace

option: mark the virtual corner with a
light, flagpole, or other addition

*Exterior cures for a missing area use fences, landscaping,
or masonry to energetically complete the space.*

If the missing area is occupied by an existing porch
or patio, add something to further define the space,
such as flower boxes along the porch railing or a
hedge to border the patio. You can even wrap a
porch railing in a string of holiday lights. By adding
a remedy or cure of your own, you apply the power
of your intention to the situation.

Missing areas can also be cured from the inside
of the house, by using a large mirror to visually
expand the interior space.

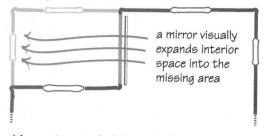

a mirror visually expands interior space into the missing area

A large mirror inside the house helps cure a missing area by reflecting the existing space outward.

If none of these options are feasible for you, another way to offset the influence of a missing area is to add feng shui enhancements (plants, wind chimes, crystals, etc.) to the corresponding area of the ba gua in each major room of the house. For example, if your home is missing part or all of the Marriage area, adding feng shui enhancements to the Marriage areas in your bedroom, living room, dining room, and kitchen will help the rebalance the space.

Irregular House Shapes

Homes with irregular outlines or that have a strong nonrectangular shape may not even come close to fitting neatly into the ba gua. While these spaces can be more interesting than a plain rectangular structure, the missing areas and extensions create unbalanced energy, which is often further destabilized by odd corners and angles.

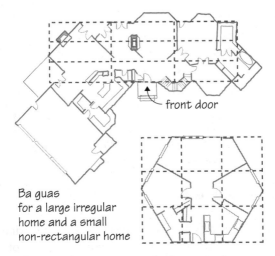

front door

Ba guas
for a large irregular
home and a small
non-rectangular home

*Very irregular or nonrectangular homes may have
unbalanced or unstable energy.*

Rather than trying to turn an odd shape into a rec-
tangle with exterior cures, the best solution for home
shapes such as these is to focus on creating the best
possible interior feng shui, using the room-by-room
guidelines coming up in the following chapters.

The Least You Need to Know

- The modern practice of orienting the ba gua
  to the doorway reflects how we experience a
  space psychologically.

- Extensions are parts of the floor plan that
  stick out from the main outline of the house;
  they tend to strengthen that area of the home.

- When parts of the home extend forward of the front door, related activities make take place away from home much of the time.

- Missing areas are like bites taken out of the floor plan; they indicate weakness in that area of the home. Both exterior and interior cures can be used to correct a missing area.

- If your home has a very irregular or non-rectangular shape, focus on creating good interior feng shui to help balance and stabilize the space.

Chapter 5

Let Chi In

In This Chapter

- Attracting good chi to the front door
- Improving the energy of the main entry
- Controlling chi flow through your home
- Correcting problems with stairs and hallways

Feng shui is about creating a positive and supportive atmosphere in your space. If chi—the vital energy that flows through all things—can't get in and move around, the energy of your home will feel stale and flat. As a result, you might feel a little stale and flat yourself—listless, lacking in enthusiasm—and wondering why life isn't just a tad more fun!

It doesn't take much to bring a dose of enlivening chi into your home and encourage it to flow smoothly throughout your space. The easy guidelines in this chapter show you how.

Welcoming Opportunities

When the chi in and around your home is strong and fresh it supports a steady flow of opportunities and new energy into your life. This in turn helps you make progress toward your goals. People who feel stuck in a dead-end job, have an unfulfilling relationship, or generally lack prosperity often live in homes where the flow of chi is blocked or restricted in some way.

Chi flows in through the front door and out through other doors and windows.

Chi should enter your home through the front door, circulate through interior spaces, and exit through secondary doors and windows. If this flow is blocked, it can show up as restrictions or lack of energy in the related aspects of your life. A little feng shui attention to your front door and other key areas can make a big difference in your ability to achieve success and happiness.

Trouble Underfoot

Chi flows along the same pathways and corridors that people use. If you can walk easily and smoothly up to the front door and through your home, chi will flow smoothly as well. Anywhere your movement is blocked and restricted, the flow of chi will also be affected.

Find out if chi can get to your home easily by walking slowly from the street to your front door. Be alert for anything that gets in your way or slows you down, such as ...

- Cracks in a cement path (fill them in).
- Uneven paving stones (reset them so they are level).
- Bushes or tree branches overhanging the path (cut them back).
- Inadequate lighting (install new or brighter lights).
- Unstable steps or handrail (fix or replace them).

- Anything that should have been put away: a
  garden hose, your kid's tricycle, that pile of
  newspapers you haven't taken to the recycling
  center yet, etc.

In addition to things that slow you down or get in
your way, anything unattractive is also a source of
sha (negative) chi. Unhealthy plants, wind-blown
trash, and rusting lawn accessories are signs that
your yard needs feng shui attention. If it's not
adding beauty, convenience, or safety, dig it out,
cover it up, or get rid of it.

Open Wide: Your "Mouth of Chi"

The front door, or *Mouth of Chi*, plays a critical role
in the feng shui of your home. When your front
door has good feng shui, it encourages a steady flow
of fresh energy and new opportunities into your
home and your life. Any feng shui problems around
the main entry will interfere with this essential function, and should be corrected as quickly as possible.

 Say "Chi"

The main entrance to your home is
called the **Mouth of Chi** because it is the
place where nourishing energy enters your
home.

Anything that gets in the way of the front door
is a feng shui no-no, so please don't use the space

behind or around it as a storage area, no matter how convenient it may seem. Here are some other easy ways to increase the energy around your Mouth of Chi:

- An exterior light beside or over the front door will help to attract chi to your home. Turn it on for a few hours every evening to keep the energy strong.

- Potted plants beside the front door, especially blooming varieties, are a good way to enhance this area.

- Increase interior lighting in a dark entryway, and turn it on for at least a couple of hours every day.

- Make sure your doormat is clean, that your doorbell works, and that any metal fixtures such as a brass knocker or house numbers are polished and shiny.

Remember, light, open, beautiful things enhance chi; heavy, dark, ugly things slow or weigh it down. Usually it's a good idea to increase chi around the entry. However, you may need to slow chi down or provide some protection if your front door is exposed to a busy street or other unsettling energy. A wind chime hung beside the door or at the top of your porch steps will help to disperse any negative or overly strong chi before it hits your front door.

> **It's Elemental** _____
>
> The Mouth of Chi is so important in feng shui that even if you normally use a different door, you should make it a point to use your front door at least once a week. If you go in and out through the garage or another door most of the time, the chi around the front door will get stale.

In our car-centric culture, many of us go in and out of our houses through the garage most of the time. However, this does not mean that the door from your garage into the house becomes the Mouth of Chi. The Mouth of Chi is always the door that the architect designed as the main entry to the home, even if you rarely use it.

If you rent part of someone else's home, or share a house or apartment with roommates, the door leading to your private space is your personal Mouth of Chi.

First Impressions Count

First impressions are important in feng shui because the first thing seen when you enter a space sets the mood for your experience there. People entering your home should be welcomed by something attractive, such as …

- A beautiful arrangement of fresh or lifelike flowers in a pretty vase.

- Works of art chosen for their specific mood. If you often feel stressed when arriving home from work, choose art for the entry that is soothing in tone, such as a tranquil landscape scene.

- A handsome piece of furniture, such as a bench, console table, or small chest of drawers. Make sure the furniture is of a size appropriate to the scale of the entry, and that it is clean and in good repair.

- A fish tank or fountain, which will help attract prosperity. Place the fountain, if you choose to use one, so the water flows toward the interior of the home.

- A photograph or poster of a waterfall, which can be used instead of a fountain, will also evoke prosperity although the effect will not be as powerful.

A very small or narrow entry will restrict the flow of chi into the rest of the house. These small spaces are usually fairly dark, so use a bright light, turn it on more often, and leave it on a little longer. Adding a large mirror to a small entry creates the impression of a larger space and also increases the brightness of the room.

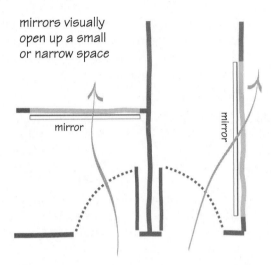

mirrors visually
open up a small
or narrow space

mirror

mirror

*Mirrors are a good solution for a small or narrow entry
because they create the impression of a larger space.*

You can enhance the effect of the mirror (if space
allows) by placing a small table or chest of drawers
in front of it. A vase of flowers or small statuette on
top of the table or chest will attract the eye and be
doubled by the mirror. Another option is to hang a
print, painting, or photograph on the wall opposite
the mirror so that both it and its reflection beautify
the space. If you do choose to use a mirror in your
entry, make sure that whatever it is reflecting is
attractive and chi-enhancing.

Moving Around

Stairways and hallways affect and direct the flow of
chi through your home. Follow the guidelines in

this section to find out if your stairs and hallways are helping or hindering the feng shui of your home.

Chi Flows Down Stairs

Chi flows like water, so when it comes to a flight of stairs it runs downhill just like a stream tumbling down a steep ravine. This means that the area at the bottom of the stairs is in the path of a fast and turbulent flow of chi. Try not to place a sofa, armchair, or desk in this area, as it will be difficult to relax or concentrate there.

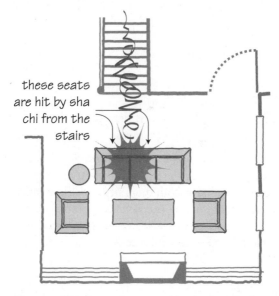

these seats are hit by sha chi from the stairs

Try to avoid sitting, eating, or working in the path of turbulent chi.

Spiral staircases also encourage a rapid downward flow of chi, which is intensified because it is concentrated in a relatively small area. This type of stairway is especially damaging in the Tai Chi (center) area of the home where it is like a hole drilled through the middle of the house. You can cure a spiral staircase by wrapping a green ribbon or a leafy garland around the railing, from the bottom of the stairs all the way to the top. A potted plant (real or lifelike) placed underneath the stairs, and a wind chime hung at the top of them, will also help to lift chi up the stairs.

In many homes, stairs leading from the main floor to higher levels begin in the foyer. When the bottom of a flight of stairs is in line with the front door, chi could be flowing down the stairs and right out of the house. This drains the home of energy, luck, and resources. The closer the stairs are to the door, the stronger the effect will be. If the distance from the door to the stairs is less than about eight or ten feet, some feng shui adjustment will be a good idea.

If there's room enough, place a basket at the bottom of stairs that end near your front door, to catch any chi that is rolling down them before it flows back out the front door. If you don't have room for a basket (or in addition to it) hang a faceted crystal ball halfway between the door and the first step. A crystal chandelier in the front hall will have the same effect; make sure that the chandelier crystals are all sparkly clean, and replace any missing or damaged ones. A light at the top of the stairs will also help to attract chi to the upper levels of the home.

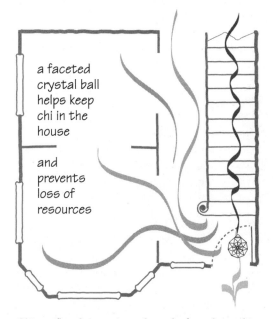

a faceted crystal ball helps keep chi in the house

and prevents loss of resources

Chi can flow down stairs and out the front door, taking your luck and money with it.

Hallways Are the Arteries of Your Home

Think of your hallways as the arteries of your home. When they are open and uncluttered, chi can flow freely. When they are blocked, the energy of your home will suffer, just as blocked arteries cause physical health problems in the body.

Take a stroll through the hallways of your home to see how freely chi can flow through them. Any place where you have to turn to the side to get around a table, junior's stroller, or that stack of boxes you've been meaning to get to, the flow of chi is constricted. Things that you bump into, trip over, or bang an elbow on are stopping the flow of chi and should be cleared out of the way.

Sha Alert! _____

If furniture or clutter is blocking your hall-ways, you may feel a sense of isolation or disconnect between the related aspects of your life, depending on which areas of the ba gua are affected.

Blocked hallways are not the only feng shui problem for these key elements of your home. Remember, in feng shui you are aiming for balance and harmony, so if chi is moving too quickly through your hall-ways, that can be an issue as well.

Long, straight hallways create a strong flow of chi toward whatever is at the far end. The longer the hallway, the stronger the effect will be. Not only does this cause sha chi at the end of the hallway, but chi may also rush past any rooms that open off the hall instead of flowing into them.

If the hallway leads from your front door through the center of the house to the back door, watch out. Not only is chi flowing straight out the back with-out circulating through the entire home, but health problems along the center line of the body can also be indicated.

faceted
crystal balls
slow down
fast-moving
chi in a
long, narrow
hallway and
redirect it
into other
spaces

Chi can flow too quickly in a long hallway.

The best way to assess the feng shui of your hallways is to pay attention to how you and your family move through them. Banged elbows, stubbed toes, or too much running are all signs that some adjustment is needed. Hang faceted crystal balls to slow down the fast-moving energy associated with a long hallway, and try to avoid working, eating, or sleeping where it will affect you.

The Least You Need to Know

- Make sure your front door opens smoothly and completely, and remove any clutter in the immediate area.

- Mirrors create the impression of a brighter, larger space, and are a good solution for a small, dark entry.

- The first thing you see when entering your home—and every room within your home—should be attractive and welcoming.

- How people move through your space provides important clues about where chi is blocked or stuck and where it might be moving too quickly.

- Faceted crystal balls are a good way to slow down fast-moving chi, and to keep chi from flowing down the stairs and out your front door.

Chapter 6

The Truth About Clutter

In This Chapter

- The feng shui perspective on clutter
- Why clutter makes you feel tired
- The many ways clutter could be affecting you
- How feng shui can help you get rid of clutter
- Do's and don'ts for clearing clutter

Have you been thinking you ought to do something about your clutter, but just can't seem to get started? You are certainly not alone, and this chapter will provide you with some motivation to get started. If you think you don't have clutter and can skip right over this chapter, you might want to read on. Clutter could be lurking in your home in unexpected forms and places.

Clutter Is Stuck Energy

Clutter is defined as anything that gets in your way or that you do not use, need, or love. It's easy to see that piles of old magazines and a 10-year supply of used paper bags are clutter, but many people are surrounded by other types of clutter without being aware of it.

Beautiful, expensive designer clothes are clutter if you never wear them (especially if they no longer fit). That valuable portrait of your great-grandfather is clutter if you don't like it and resent it hanging in a prominent spot in your living room. And your collection of antique beer mugs is clutter if it's stashed in a box in the back of the garage where you trip over it every time you take out the trash.

Even your neatnik neighbor could be living with secret clutter. Tidy, well-organized people sometimes have lots of tidy, well-organized clutter; it may be neatly in its place, but it is blocking chi nonetheless if there's no good reason to keep it in the first place.

From a feng shui perspective, all kinds of clutter are both a cause and a symptom of stuck energy. You learned in the previous chapter about the importance of creating a smooth flow of chi through your home. When your home is filled with clutter—even beautiful, expensive clutter—chi can't circulate and the energy in your space will become stagnant.

The more clutter you have, the more sluggish the energy in your home becomes and the more difficult it is for fresh chi to get in. This encourages more and more clutter to pile up, and makes it harder and harder for you to get energized to do something about it.

Feng Fact

Many people discover that when they finally get rid of their clutter, they also lose some weight—without consciously trying. (How great is that?) This doesn't surprise folks who know about feng shui; they recognize that stuck energy in your home leads to stuck energy in your body. When the home clutter is released, the physical clutter of unwanted pounds starts to dissipate as well.

Getting rid of your clutter frees up an immense amount of energy and enables fresh, vital chi to flow in and fill your home. When there's room for new chi to come in, there's room for new ideas, new projects, new people, and new activities and experiences, too. Just about any positive change you want to encourage through feng shui can be doubly energized by getting rid of clutter.

How Clutter Affects You

Clutter is disempowering on many levels. When our homes are filled with clutter, we are likely to feel tired, depressed, indecisive, ineffective, creatively blocked, unable to focus, overly emotional, or too lethargic to care.

Everything that surrounds you should be working for you in some way. If you are not satisfied with how you feel, how much energy you have, or with your ability to succeed in your career, attract a good relationship, or prosper financially, there's a good chance clutter is part of the problem.

Clutter in and Around the House

In feng shui terms, anything that is neglected, unwanted, or unappealing will drag your energy down every time you look at it. Are the things in your space supporting you and contributing to the positive quality of your life, or are they making it harder for you to reach your goals and live out your dreams? Here are some specific ways that clutter in your home could be weighing you down.

How you care for your kitchen is a clue to whether you are giving proper attention to your own nourishment and sources of abundance. When clutter is allowed to take over the kitchen, that's a sign that it's time to bring home, work, and family life into better balance.

Clutter can turn social spaces like the living room and dining room into dens of isolation, especially if the mess is so bad that you've stopped inviting friends over for dinner. If your dining table is so covered with clutter that your family never eats there, it could be contributing to a lack of connection or communication among family members.

Clutter in your bedroom can make it hard to get going in the morning, and not just because you can't find that pink sweater you were planning to wear today. All that stuck energy will literally make it hard to pry yourself out of bed.

It's Elemental

Getting rid of bedroom clutter makes room for new love relationships, so if you've been feeling lonely, go clean out a dresser drawer with the intention that it will soon be filled with your new partner's things!

Clutter in your office makes it hard to concentrate and get work done, slows down your projects, and prevents opportunities from flowing in. Hoping for that promotion? Clearing all old information from your file drawers and hard drive will create space for those new responsibilities you want to prove you can handle.

Clutter in the Attic, Basement, and Garage

Attics represent your future aspirations. Any kind of overhead clutter can weigh you down and make it difficult to feel optimistic about the future. Clear out everything but the things you really treasure, and store what you decide to keep so it is neat and tidy.

Basements represent your subconscious, which can be a scary concept; who knows what you will find in those often dank, dark spaces? Unresolved issues from the past reside down there, so be courageous and clean out your basement clutter.

If your home doesn't have an attic or basement, chances are good that you've filled your garage with all kinds of stuff because you just don't know what else to do with it. In feng shui terms, this is not a good idea, because your car represents mobility and self-direction. Clutter in the garage slows you down in all kinds of ways. Clearing out your garage restores your freedom of movement on both literal and symbolic levels.

Many homes these days are built with three- or even four-car garages, in expectation that at least one of those bays will be used to store your barbecue grill, bicycles, recycling bins, and sports equipment. This is a great idea, so long as the car areas are kept clear for your cars, and the storage areas are tidy and well organized. Don't let stored clutter take over the entire space.

Living clutter-free does not mean creating a sterile, minimalist environment; it means getting rid of the excess so that everything around you is there for a reason. A good decluttering helps loosen up stuck chi and creates space for new energy to flow into your life. The physical space you free up creates mental and spiritual space for you to discover and pursue your true path in life and define who you want to become.

Feng Shui Secrets for Clearing Clutter

In Chapter 5 you learned the importance of removing clutter from around the front door, your Mouth of Chi, so make sure that area gets priority attention. The Tai Chi—the physical center of your home—should be your second priority for clutter clearing.

Because the Tai Chi connects all the different sections of the ba gua, it affects every aspect of your life. Clutter in the Tai Chi will contribute to low or difficult energy throughout the home; it is important to do what you can to keep this important area clean, well lit, tidy, and attractive to all the senses.

Once you have addressed the Tai Chi of your home, see how much space you can create in the center of each room as well. In an extremely cluttered home, this simple change can help make space for the new energy you'll need to tackle the rest of the mess.

Use the ba gua to decide which areas to tackle next. Look for your worst clutter accumulations, and see what areas of the ba gua they could be affecting. Any gua that is related to an aspect of life in which you feel stuck or unable to make progress could probably use some clutter-clearing attention.

It's Elemental

Red, which represents the fire element, is a very energizing color. Wear red while you tackle your clutter to help keep your energy up and your enthusiasm high.

If you are really having trouble tackling a particular clutter area, try ringing a bell, shaking a rattle, or banging a gong over it. Loud sound vibrations help shake up stuck energy, and are a feng shui technique for clearing stale chi from a space. Don't have any bells or rattles in the house? Give your three-year-old a pot lid and a wooden spoon to hit it with, and encourage him to make as much noise as he wants wherever you have piles of stuff that should be cleared away.

The defeat, fatigue, and depression that most of us feel when we think about our clutter will usually evaporate as soon as you put yourself in action. The more clutter-clearing you do, the more energized and enthusiastic you will feel and the easier it will be to keep going.

More Tips for Successful Clutter Clearing

The following guidelines will help you get off to a successful start with your clutter clearing and stay with it long enough to really see results.

Do ...

- Start today, and commit to spending 5 to 10 minutes every day on some kind of clutter-clearing task.

- Create a "Clutter Free Zone" where you can relax and get away from the mess while you work on the rest of your home.

- Focus on one room (bathroom, kitchen, bedroom) or on one type of clutter (clothes, books, photos, papers) at a time. Count a seriously cluttered closet as a separate room.

- Remember that baby steps are okay. If you have a lot of energy and momentum and want to keep at it all day, that's terrific. On the days you don't feel like that (and there may be a lot of them), it's fine to do just a little bit at a time.

- Be decisive. If you don't know where to start, go to your most cluttered space and find three things that you can throw out or give away. Now remove those items from that space, and put them in the trash or in a "donations" box or bag.

- Always ask yourself, "Could someone else use this?" and "Can this be recycled?" before throwing anything away.

- Make sure you have done a thorough decluttering before you buy any additional storage boxes or organizing systems. If you do a good job getting rid of clutter, you might not need them.

- Recognize that coping with your clutter may cause hidden emotional issues to rise to the surface. Decluttering your kitchen may force you to confront food issues, for example. Going through your late Mom's things can bring up feelings of loss and sadness. Getting rid of clothes may involve accepting the fact that you will never, ever be a size six again.

If difficult emotions do come up during your clutter clearing, allow that to happen even if it feels uncomfortable. Once you let the feelings out, it can be much easier to let go of that clutter.

Feng Fact

Donating your unwanted items to charity instead of adding them to your local landfill is good for the environment, which is good feng shui. Clothes can go to the Salvation Army, Goodwill, and women's or homeless shelters. Toys and sports equipment can be given to Boys & Girls Clubs, youth groups, or Big Brother/Big Sister organizations. Animal shelters will be happy to have your worn towels and blankets, and nursing homes and libraries welcome books and magazines.

Don't ...

- Feel guilty about having clutter, or for having given up on past clutter-clearing efforts before completion. Clutter is normal, and no matter how bad your clutter problem is, someone somewhere has clutter that is worse (much, much worse) than your own.

- Put off clutter clearing until some hoped-for future date when you will miraculously have all the time and energy you need to clear out your clutter in one massive effort. This will never happen!

- Expect to clear out years (or decades) of clutter in one weekend. It took a long time for that stuff to pile up, and it will take awhile to get through all of it.

- Create more than one "undecided" box. It's okay to set aside a few things that you are really not sure about yet; it's not okay to use the "undecided" label to avoid making the decisions that will get that clutter out of your house.

- Keep anything just because "it might come in handy someday." It might not, and in the meantime a whole lot of todays and tomorrows will be unnecessarily cluttered by it. Trust that if you really do need three dozen empty margarine tubs 10 years from now, more will be available to you.

- Feel guilty about giving away or selling something of value that someone else gave you as a gift. Keep the love and affection that came with the gift (which doesn't take up any space at all except in your heart), and choose to release the clutter.

- Assume that holding a yard sale or posting dozens (or hundreds) of items on eBay are the best ways to get rid of things. Sure, you could make some money, but will it be worth the time and effort? A yard sale is great if you really want the cash; if you just want to feel you got some value from that stuff, donate it to charity. Get a receipt for your donation and claim the tax deduction to which you are entitled.

Finally, if you need help coping with your clutter, don't feel you have to do it alone. Hire a professional organizer to guide and encourage you, or explore the many clutter-clearing resources available on the Internet. (Appendix B is a good place to start.)

The Least You Need to Know

- Anything you don't use, need, or love is clutter, regardless of what it looks like or how valuable it might be.

- Getting rid of clutter is a great way to shift stuck energy and create space for new relationships and experiences in your life.

- Sound vibrations from bells, rattles, and gongs can help your clutter-clearing efforts by shaking loose some of that stuck energy.

- Your front door—the Mouth of Chi—and the physical center of your home—the Tai Chi—should get priority clutter-clearing attention.

Chapter 7

Ouch! What Was That?

In This Chapter

- How negative energy affects you
- Common sources of outdoor and indoor "secret arrows"
- Other forms of harmful chi
- Feng shui remedies and protections

Not all chi is good chi. Identifying and then removing, correcting, or protecting against "sha chi" (negative energy) is an important aspect of feng shui. In this chapter, you will learn more about common forms of negative energy that could be affecting your home, what causes them, and what to do about them.

Watch Out for Secret Arrows

One of the most harmful kinds of sha chi is *secret arrows*. When you sit, work, eat, or sleep in the path of secret arrows, your personal chi is under attack. This can result in increased stress and irritability, headaches, or other physical ailments, depending on what part of the body might be affected.

> ### Say "Chi"
>
> **Secret arrows** (also called "poison arrows") are invisible daggers of harmful energy created by pointed objects, sharp corners, and narrow edges.

Because the effects of secret arrows can be subtle (although potentially very damaging over the long term) you may not be consciously aware of them.

Secret Arrows Outside the House

Secret arrows outside your home can affect the energy of a particular room, or even of the entire house. A secret arrow aimed at your front door is extremely harmful; it weakens the Mouth of Chi and attacks you each time you enter or leave your home.

Check for secret arrows outside your home by looking outward from the front door and from each side of the house (either by standing in your yard or looking through windows) for any corner of a building or roof that points at your home. This could be a neighboring structure, or even your own garage or a garden shed.

(view from above)

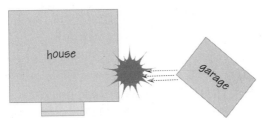

secret arrows from the corner
of the garage are hitting the
side of this house

*The corners of nearby structures can send secret arrows
of sha chi at your home.*

The taller and closer the corner or angle is, the
stronger its impact will be. A good guideline is to
assume that secret arrows are harmful to a distance
equal to the height of the source. For example, the
corner of a 30-foot building will send out secret
arrows of sha chi for a distance of approximately
30 feet.

Secret arrows can be caused by anything sharp or
pointed, such as a dead tree branch that looks like
an accusing finger pointed at the side of your
house, the lower edge of a metal awning over your
front door, or even the corners of the square posts
holding up your porch roof. When you start to
look for secret arrows, it's easy to see them every-
where and become overly concerned. Keep in mind
that …

- Secret arrows are quite accurate; they only affect what is exactly in line with them. If it's pointed in your general direction, but not directly at you, don't worry about it.

- The farther the source of the secret arrows is from you, the weaker the impact will be.

- The longer you are exposed to secret arrows, the more harmful they are. A sharp corner that you walk past several times a day is no big deal; secret arrows aimed at the outside wall beside your bed require some kind of cure or protection.

The best solution to secret arrows is to remove the source or move yourself out of harm's way. That's often impossible or impractical, so the next best remedy is to place some kind of a buffer between you and it. Anything that interrupts the stream of sha chi will do. If sha chi is aimed at a window, you can deflect it with a faceted crystal ball hung inside the window.

Plants, including bushes and trees, provide good protection from exterior secret arrows, although you may find that they don't do as well as the ones in other parts of your yard. Try to match the scale of what you are planting to the size of the problem. To blunt the sha chi from the corner of your neighbor's house just 12 feet from your kitchen wall, you'll want to plant a tree that will grow at least 8 to 10 feet high. The edges of those square support posts on the porch can be softened with ivy or potted or hanging plants.

A tree between the house and garage acts as a buffer; the faceted crystal inside the window deflects sha chi

Trees can protect you from the harmful effects of secret arrows.

It's Elemental

When using plants as protection against secret arrows—or for any other feng shui purpose—keep in mind that evergreen varieties are best. Trees or shrubs that drop their leaves in winter will be less effective.

Other ways to disrupt or absorb minor or moderate secret arrow chi outside the house include placing a fountain or other water feature, a wind chime, or large boulders where they will absorb or deflect the sha chi. For severe sha chi, use a ba gua mirror (see Chapter 2). Remember, though, that a ba gua mirror reflects sha chi back at the source, so be careful what you aim it at. If there's a chance that by deflecting the negative energy away from your home you might be sending it toward someone else's house, you might want to choose a different cure instead. (See the section "Difficult Neighbors" at the end of this chapter for more.)

Secret Arrows Inside the House

Secret arrows are also a problem where they occur inside the home. Interior corners that stick out into a room are just like the corner of a neighboring building outside: They send a stream of negative energy at whatever is in front of them. If that's your desk, couch, bed, dining table, or stove, you'll want to take corrective measures described in the next section.

Your furniture and furnishings can also create secret arrows. If you've ever bruised your shin on the sharp corner of a glass or metal coffee table, you've experienced sha chi in action.

 It's Elemental

In feng shui, furniture with rounded edges and corners is preferred; smooth shapes mean a smoother flow of chi around them, and they don't create secret arrows.

Other things to watch out for include …

- Shelves or cabinets with sharp corners or edges.

- Levelor-type window blinds (both vertical and horizontal styles), unless they are closed or raised completely; that row of narrow edges is like a row of knife edges that send cutting chi at whatever is in front of them.

- Ceiling fans; the spinning blades send cutting chi onto whatever is beneath them.

As always, pay special attention to anything near where you work, sleep, or eat. For example, if you are having trouble sleeping or often wake up in the morning with a headache, look to see if a bookcase, dresser or nightstand has an edge or corner that points at your head while you are asleep.

Protecting Yourself Against Sha Chi

Often, repositioning the furniture by a couple of inches so it is no longer in the path of the sha chi will take care of the problem. If you can't move the furniture, create some kind of a buffer or use a faceted crystal ball or wind chime to disperse the negative chi. Houseplants can be placed in front of a sharp corner, for example, and a table cover softens the edges of that nightstand beside your bed.

Photographs and artwork of things that look like secret arrows can be just as harmful as the real thing, so take a closer look at the imagery in key areas of your home. These kinds of hidden secret arrows are easy to cure: Just take them down or hang them somewhere else where they won't do any harm.

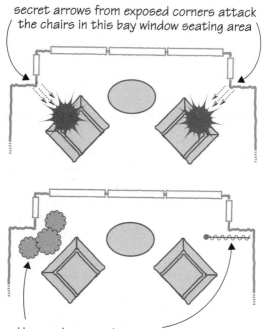

secret arrows from exposed corners attack the chairs in this bay window seating area

House plants and curtains are two ways to protect these chairs from sha chi

Protect yourself from interior sha chi with fabric, plants, faceted crystal balls or wind chimes.

Exposed beams are another common source of interior sha chi, creating pressure on whatever is underneath them. A single beam over a key area such as your bed, couch, or dining table, is a potentially serious feng shui problem that should be corrected. Many smaller beams at regular intervals across the length of the room are actually less serious because the downward pressure, although still present, is more evenly dispersed.

Again, the best and often easiest remedy is to move your furniture so that it is not directly under a beam. If that is impossible, add something to symbolically lift the energy under the beam in order to ease the downward pressure that it exerts. Some possible options are …

- Angel or bird images or figurines attached to the side of the beam.
- Uplights under the ends of the beam.
- A string of miniature lights along the sides or underside of the beam.
- Small faceted crystal balls hung from the underside of the beam. Three is a powerful number in feng shui (as is any multiple of three), so use three, six, or nine crystals for the best effect.
- Chinese bamboo flutes hung on the side of the beam.

If you choose to use bamboo flutes, it is important that they be hung at an angle so that higher ends point toward each other. If the growth direction of the bamboo is obvious, hang the flutes with the larger, older section at the bottom and the mouthpiece at the top; if you can't tell which is the older end, hang the flutes with the mouthpieces at the bottom.

The electric appliances that bring so much convenience and comfort to modern living cause a modern form of sha chi: electro-magnetic frequencies (EMF). Never sleep with the head of your bed positioned where there is a fuse box or major appliance—such as the refrigerator or stove—on the other side of the wall.

Feng Fact

The science of creating healthy homes with environmentally safe building materials and furnishings goes hand-in-hand with good feng shui. "Bau-biologie" (house biology) originated in Europe and is increasingly popular in the United States, especially for those with multiple-chemical sensitivities and other forms of immune-system distress. Careful attention to EMF levels and interior air quality are fundamental to this practice.

Make sure that any place where you spend a lot of time—such as at your desk—is well away from strong EMF influences. You are most vulnerable when you are sleeping, as that is when your body repairs and renews itself on a cellular level, but it's wise to be cautious during your waking hours as well.

Find Things That Need Fixing

Anything that doesn't work the way it should, or doesn't work at all anymore, is a sign of deteriorating chi. What kind of impact it will have on you depends on the item or appliance and its symbolic implications. For example, a broken clock in your Marriage area may indicate that you can't find the time to give your relationship the attention it deserves.

Take a look around your home to see whether all of the clocks in your house are set to different times (or not set at all: Is something somewhere still blinking "12:00"?). If all your timepieces show different times, there's a good chance that your own energy is unfocused and out of alignment in some way. Reset your clocks so they all agree with each other and see if something else in your life starts feeling more agreeable as well.

Lights, which enable you to see what's going on, symbolize insight and understanding. Burned-out light bulbs and lights that don't work in a particular area of your home imply a lack of insight into the related area of your life, depending on what part of the ba gua is being left in the dark.

Doors that stick, locks that require finicky key jiggling, and knobs that are either too stiff or too wiggly all make it harder for you to get what you want out of life. You may feel …

- That you can't "get a handle on" a situation.
- "Locked out" of important discussions or decisions.
- Frustrated that "doors won't open" for you in your professional or financial endeavors.

When these problems occur at the front door, they can affect all aspects of your life. When other doors are involved, look at the room and area of the ba gua where the door is located for insight about how your life may be impacted. For example …

- Problems with a bedroom door or in the Marriage area can affect your love life.

- If the door to your office doesn't open smoothly, you may find that new business opportunities are not flowing your way or that it is difficult to respond to them in a timely manner.

- A loose doorknob in your Wealth area could mean you can't seem to grasp the details of a financial situation.

- Kitchen cabinets that don't open easily could indicate a lack of attention to proper nourishment.

It's Elemental

Doors are all about access. If you want easy access to the good things in life, go around your house and oil all squeaky hinges, tighten any loose doorknobs, and clear out the clutter from behind all your doors.

Windows that are hard to open or that have remained closed all winter trap chi in the house. When the air in your house gets stale and stuffy, that's a sure sign that the chi is stale as well. And when stale energy can't get out, there's no room for new energy to come in. Opening all of your windows at least a little bit from time to time is especially important in a house or apartment that has only one exterior door. Visualize all the old chi flowing out of your house and fresh new chi blowing in.

Eliminate Sources of Conflict

In general, any form of sha chi or secret arrows will increase stress and tension, and that can lead to increased disagreement and arguments among the people in the home. One specific source of conflict is the situation known as "fighting doors." These are doors that bump into each other when opened.

Fighting doors could lead to arguments in this kitchen

Doors that clash when opened can lead to clashes between the people in your home.

The location of the doors often indicates what the resulting arguments are about. For example, fighting doors in the Wealth area can lead to arguments about money; in the bedroom they can cause conflict in your love relationship; in the Career area or in your office they can lead to conflicts at work, and so on.

To cure fighting doors, you can …

- Cut a length of red string to a multiple of nine inches (36", 45", 54", etc.) that is long enough to connect both doorknobs when the doors are fully closed. Tie one end of the string to each doorknob, then cut it in the middle and wrap the loose ends around the doorknob shafts.

- Hang a red tassel from each doorknob.

- Put a small red dot in the center of each door with the intention that it will enable the doors to "see" each other. Use red nail polish, paint, or a self-adhesive color-coding dot for this cure.

 It's Elemental _____

Red is the strongest, most active color (remember that it is associated with fire, the most active of the five elements), so including something red, such as the string, tassels, and dots prescribed for fighting doors, can help make your feng shui cures more powerful.

Check your closet doors, too. Closets keep things out of sight; if your bedroom door "fights" a closet door, the real reason for the conflicts in your relationship could be that one of you is protecting a secret. Or the conflict itself could be hidden; you might think everything is just fine while your partner is nurturing a secret resentment.

Water Fights Fire

Fire and water are natural enemies. Water puts out fire, but lots of fire can turn water into steam. If the kitchen stove (fire) and sink (water) are across from each other on opposite sides of the room, conflicts and arguments may frequently erupt in the kitchen.

The feng shui solution is to introduce the wood element to absorb the water chi and nurture fire. This is a much more harmonious arrangement, and can easily be created by using wood element imagery, objects, or colors, such as …

- Placing a green area rug in the space between the sink or stove.
- Adding a green plant (preferably living, but lifelike artificial is okay) on a table or counter between the sink and stove.
- Hanging a green dishtowel in front of the sink or from the oven door handle.

Keep in mind that a wooden table in the center of room will not be strong enough to cure this situation because it is not made from living wood. If you have a table in this position, place a small potted plant, a green tablecloth, or any other green or wood-energy object on the table to strengthen the desired effect.

Wood can also be used to soften the relationship between a sink and stove that are next to each other, or if your dishwasher or refrigerator is opposite or next to the stove. While the refrigerator is not considered a water-energy object, its cooling effect will also fight with fire.

Difficult Neighbors

If you aren't getting along with your neighbors, don't rush to assume it's entirely their fault (even though it might be). Take a look around to make sure that you aren't sending any secret arrows their way from your home or yard. Remove or soften any potential sources of sha chi that could be affecting the folks next door, and you may find that the tensions between you soften as well.

Sha Alert!

Although ba gua mirrors are very effective against exterior sha chi, it's not a good idea to use them when the problem is your neighbors themselves. Mirrors reflect things, and the last thing you need to do is bounce all that negative energy right back at them; it will just make the problem worse.

Enlightened feng shui-ers will send their obnoxious neighbors positive energy instead of curses, with the understanding that blessings are more powerful than anger in the long run. If you are comfortable dialoguing with a higher power, ask that your neighbors be blessed with an irresistible job offer or other good fortune that prompts them to move to another city (or at least a different neighborhood) and gets them out of your hair.

If good luck wishes are more than you can muster up for these irksome folks, hang a smiling sun face, angel, or even a guardian figure of some kind on the side of your house that faces them, and try not to entertain too many nasty thoughts. Thoughts have energy, and energy is what feng shui is all about.

The Least You Need to Know

- Anything that looks as if it could hurt you physically may be harming you energetically; don't eat, sleep, or work close to sharp edges, hard angles, or pointed objects.
- Exposed beams and ceiling fans create negative energy overhead.
- Soften the impact of "secret arrows" from sharp edges and corners with fabric or houseplants.
- Doors that bump into each other when opened can lead to arguments and conflict.
- Mirrors reflect negative energy back at the source; in dealing with difficult neighbors it's better to send positive energy instead.

The Heart of the Home

In This Chapter

- Tips and guidelines for good kitchen feng shui
- How your kitchen affects your health
- How your kitchen affects your finances
- Sources of sha chi in the kitchen, and what you can do about them

The kitchen is sometimes called "the heart of the home," and with good reason; in ancient cultures the hearth was a sacred place representing the life-giving sustenance of Earth's bounty. Feng shui recognizes the kitchen as one of the most important rooms in the house because it is where we connect with the energies that nourish us physically (food), financially (money), and emotionally (family). In this chapter, you'll learn quick and easy ways to make sure you and your family are enjoying the benefits of good kitchen feng shui.

Creating Good Chi in the Kitchen

As a focal point for family life, the kitchen has a central role in our lives. It is often the first space we enter when we come home and where we set down the burdens that we've brought with us, from groceries to school backpacks, briefcases, or an armload of mail. Feng shui reminds us to see the kitchen not just as where we put the groceries away and dish up dinner, but also as a place where we receive blessings and express gratitude for the gifts of life, health, and prosperity.

Feng Shui Colors for the Kitchen

The kitchen should be bright and sunny in feeling, evoking the warmth of the sun and hearth. Reds and earth tones are good here, while green accents add wood energy to feed the stove's fire, and touches of purple help to support prosperity. Sometimes a small change is all that's needed. For example, three bright red apples on the counter of an all-white kitchen become the visual focal point of the room, bringing warmth and living energy into a cool, impersonal space.

Dark, cramped kitchens can be transformed with warm white or pale yellow paint, brighter light fixtures, and cheerful accessories that bring reds and yellows into the room. A kitchen with lots of black and chrome appliances and fixtures will benefit from touches of green, purple, and red to support health and prosperity.

Healthy Eating

Living plants are a wonderful way to bring the energy of health and vitality to your kitchen. A sunny windowsill—especially a window near the sink—is the perfect place for a row of herbs in little pots. If your kitchen doesn't have enough space or natural light for live plants, include something else to bring that energy in on a symbolic level, such as:

- Wallpaper, window curtains, dishtowels, or oven mitts with a design featuring plants, vegetables, or fruit
- Artwork representing edible plants or fruit
- Ceramic tiles or trivets with a vine or floral design
- Refrigerator magnets shaped like vegetables or fruit
- A lifelike artificial plant beside the sink or on top of the refrigerator

When you come home from the store and put your groceries away, think about the health and vitality these foods will bring to you and your family. As you reach for a snack or prepare a meal, take a moment to focus on how fortunate you are to have this nourishment at your fingertips. Visualize your kitchen always filled with nature's bounty, and say a quiet "thank you" for the food that sustains you and your family. This moment of awareness and gratitude will help to keep the chi of your kitchen supportive and strong.

It's Elemental

Keep kitchen canisters and other containers more than half-full as much as possible. Every time you see these containers, your subconscious mind will register plenty rather than the implied lack created by an almost empty jar. Get in the habit of restocking your food supplies before you run low, and you will fill your kitchen with the energy of abundance.

One easy way to improve the chi of the kitchen is to make sure that everything involved in food preparation and serving is attractive and pleasant to work with. If you are cooking with pots that you don't like, eating from dishes that you do not love, or using paper towels for napkins because the good ones are put away in the back of a closet, each seemingly minor incident is detracting from your ability to enjoy and benefit from your meals.

Get rid of the stuff you never use, start using the things you love, and fill your kitchen with accessories that you really enjoy. This is feng shui in action, and it's a wonderful way to transform the energy of your kitchen so you can receive the support and comfort that the heart of your home should provide.

Cooking Up Prosperity

Feng shui reminds us that in order to prosper, we need to be healthy. The feng shui of your kitchen—especially the stove—can have a big influence on your financial situation, even if you rarely or never cook.

Put Your Wealth Generator to Work

In feng shui, the stove is your "wealth generator." It is the most important symbolic factor in your ability to prosper financially, so make sure it works the way it should. Any problems with the stove can indicate problems with money or limitations to your ability to bring home a good income. A burner that doesn't heat could be a sign of fruitless effort, and an oven that runs too hot could be burning up your money. Dirt and grime are also signs of sha chi (negative energy), so be sure to keep your stovetop and oven clean.

 Feng Fact

The association of the stove with wealth stems from the belief that when the kitchen has poor feng shui, the cook will be tense and distracted. Poorly prepared food will undermine our health, and without physical strength it is more difficult to earn a good living. Good feng shui in the kitchen supports healthful cooking, healthful meals keep us strong, and when we are strong we can work hard and earn lots of money.

One easy way to activate money chi is to use your stovetop at least once a day, rather than always relying on the microwave to boil water for tea or heat up a cup of soup. Vary which burner you use, so that all are used regularly. If you don't use your stove, or use the same one burner all the time, symbolically you are limiting your ability to benefit from financial resources.

When the stovetop is not in use, put all pots and pans away. Unused pots stored on top of the stove can squash prosperity chi, especially when they cover the rear left burner. If you visualize the ba gua over the stovetop, with Career in the center front, the rear left burner is in the Wealth position.

Keep the Stove Area Strong

The stove is such an important feature in feng shui that the entire area around it should get special attention. This means removing or protecting against anything that could weaken the chi of this area of the kitchen.

Things hanging over the stove create oppressive chi that could suppress your finances (you do want your money to grow, right?). A hanging pot rack is a feng shui no-no if it is directly over the stove, and a shelf of large or heavy items will weigh down this important area. If you can't remove a built-in feature over the stove, such as a cabinet or hood, hang a small wind chime or faceted crystal from it to lift the chi above the stove.

Prosperity Chi Throughout the Kitchen

Take a look at your floor plan to see which gua your kitchen is in. A kitchen in the Wealth area of your home is especially fortunate, and will benefit from lots of green and purple accents and living plants. You can also activate money chi by working with the Wealth area within the room.

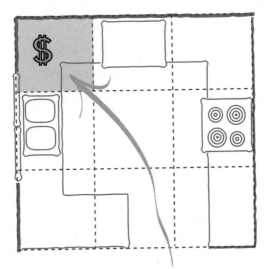

To support prosperity, place something that symbolizes wealth or abundance in the Wealth area of your kitchen.

A pretty basket or bowl of fresh fruit represents abundance. If you can place that fruit bowl in the Wealth area of the kitchen, it will have an even stronger effect. Yes, you are allowed to eat the fruit, but don't let the bowl sit empty; aim to keep at least three pieces of fruit in the bowl at all times. Purple and green grapes are especially good abundance symbols for the wealth area.

> **It's Elemental**
>
> Purple is the color most closely associated with wealth in feng shui. Add purple to the Wealth area of your kitchen if you want to increase prosperity.

If you don't have room for a fruit bowl in the kitchen Wealth area, some other options are:

- Artwork of fruit on the wall
- A green or purple trivet or other accent on the wall or counter
- A bowl or jar of loose change in a cabinet in that area

The possibilities are limitless, and include any kind of imagery that symbolizes wealth to you.

Sha Chi in the Kitchen

Although we have talked about the symbolic meaning of the kitchen as the "heart of the home," it is not good for the kitchen to be located in the physical center (the tai chi) of the house. This area of the ba gua is strongly associated with health; when the kitchen is in the center its strong fire energy can lead to health problems along the centerline of the body, aggravate heart conditions, and cause problems with digestion.

If your kitchen is in the center of the home, hang a large faceted crystal in the center of the room, paint the walls yellow, and place objects representing earth energy—such as large stones, natural crystals, or ceramic objects—in each corner of the room.

If your stove is positioned against a wall, look to see what's on the other side. A toilet or sink on the other side of the wall from your stove symbolically puts out the stove's fire with water energy. This weakens both the prosperity and the nourishing energy associated with the stove, and may indicate difficulty receiving full nourishment from your food.

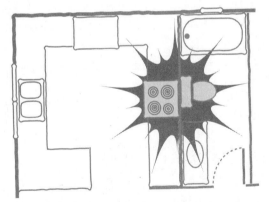

The nourishing fire energy of the stove can be extinguished by a sink, tub, shower, or toilet on the other side of the wall.

To correct this situation, you can:

- Paint the wall behind the plumbing fixture green

- Hang artwork of bamboo or other green trees above the plumbing fixture

- Place a mirror on the kitchen wall above the stove

The green paint brings in wood energy, which absorbs the water of the plumbing fixture, and feeds the stove's fire. The mirror visually pushes the kitchen space back through the bathroom wall. If you can hang the mirror so it reflects the stove burners, that's even better, because visually doubling the stovetop symbolically doubles your money. You can use all of these methods, or choose one or two that work with your home layout and décor.

It is also important to be alert to sources of sha chi within the kitchen itself, and to protect the stove and the cook from any kind of secret arrows. Refer to Chapter 7 for guidelines on what to look out for and how to correct it.

Cook from the Command Position

Using the *Command Position* is an important feng shui guideline for all important activities, especially cooking, eating, work, and sleeping.

Even if the only cooking you do involves opening a take-out container or pushing buttons on the microwave, it is important to evaluate the position of your stove. In order for the cook to be in the Command Position, the stove must be built into a cooking island or counter extension.

Say "Chi"

In the **Command Position** you face into the room with a clear view of the entrance and a solid wall behind you for support. The best location is often diagonally opposite the entrance. The Command Position puts you in control of your space, and of those aspects in your life that are affected by that space.

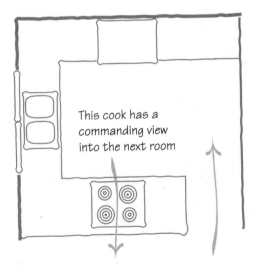

This cook has a commanding view into the next room

Cooking from the Command Position supports health and prosperity.

Unfortunately, it is more common, especially in a small kitchen, for the stove to be installed against a wall, so the cook has his/her back to the room while cooking.

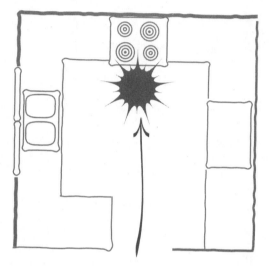

A stove that faces the wall places the cook in a vulnerable position.

This is a vulnerable position, in which the cook could be easily startled. Being startled is not a good thing when working with fire, hot oil, boiling water, etc. If the entrance to the kitchen is directly in line with the stove, the situation is even more serious; this stove position is thought to lead to an increase in accidents for the occupants of the home.

If you must cook with your back to the room, here are some steps you can take for feng shui protection:

- Hang a large mirror on the wall above the stove, so that you can see what's going on behind you as you cook.

- Place a guardian image (a saint, deity, or favorite animal or bird) on the opposite side of the room where it can "watch your back" for you.

- Hang a faceted crystal ball halfway between the stove and the kitchen doorway to interrupt the flow of chi from the door to the stove.

The Command Position is also important for a home office or home administration center in the kitchen. If you sit facing the wall, place a mirror where you will be able to see the room behind you. This mirror does not have to be very large, as long as it enables you to see anyone who might be approaching behind you.

As you place any of these cures or enhancements in your kitchen, visualize all residents of the house communicating with kindness, patience and tolerance, and hold in your heart the strong intention that every member of the family will be happy, healthy, and prosperous.

The Least You Need to Know

- Even a modern, high-tech kitchen should include some natural chi in the form of fresh fruit, living plants, or images of trees and flowers.

- The condition of your stove reflects the state of your finances; make sure it is clean and in good working order, even if you never cook.

- If your stove is not in the Command Position, hang a mirror on the wall above the stove so you can see behind you as you cook.

Chapter 9

The Art of Dining

In This Chapter

- Improving chi flow in the dining room
- Creating a peaceful dining atmosphere
- Family dinners are good feng shui

In ancient cultures, "breaking bread" together, whether as a family or with strangers, was an honored way to build community. More recently, potluck dinners, pancake breakfasts, and company picnics have continued this tradition.

We haven't done so well at maintaining this important ritual in our homes, however. Today, the dining room is often one of the most neglected rooms in the house; either it is a formal space that is rarely used, or it has been taken over for use as a home office or projects space. Busy schedules and multiple-careers can make it almost impossible for families to share dinner together on a regular basis. From a feng shui perspective, we are missing out on an important and once-sacred aspect of life. This chapter presents some ways you can remedy that.

Creating Good Chi in the Dining Room

Not every home has a formal dining room, but if yours does I recommend that you use it as often as is practical. Many beautifully (sometimes very expensively) furnished dining rooms are used only on holidays or other special occasions. That means this lovely room is left unused much of the time. When a room is rarely used, the energy in that space will be low, no matter how attractive, well lit, or airy it is.

So often when we think about feng shui we focus on the physical items that we are adding to or removing from a space, forgetting that the lively chi of our own presence and activity is an important factor as well. The best way to raise the energy in your dining room is to eat dinner there at least several times a week.

It may seem easier just to plop down at the kitchen table or breakfast nook when dinner time rolls around, but how many steps further is it to dining room, really? If your dining room is free of clutter it should hardly take any effort at all to make sitting down to dinner one of the nicest and most relaxing parts of your day.

Clutter in the Dining Room

A cramped dining room can create a feeling of pressure in family relationships and interfere with good digestion. Too much heavy, dark, old furniture—especially when it is squeezed into too small a space—also creates a heavy, dark feeling and blocks the flow of chi. Boxes and bags of clutter have a similar effect. The older the clutter, the more stuck the energy will feel.

De-cluttering your dining room is an important first step in improving the feng shui of this space. If you have a serious clutter problem in the dining room, make clearing off the table (and keeping it clear!) your first priority. Once that's done you can move on to clearing out the sideboard drawers and dealing with that stack of boxes in the corner.

Chi Flow

The flow of chi in the dining room should be gentle but not stagnant. It's good to have two doors or entrances to the dining room to allow chi to circulate, but if doorways on opposite walls are directly in line with each other, chi will move straight through the room too quickly. A faceted crystal ball or crystal chandelier over the center of the dining table will help to balance chi in the room, and also helps people with eating disorders embrace healthier habits.

A mirror is also helpful for improving chi flow in the dining room. Make sure that the mirror reflects something attractive: a nice piece of furniture, a pleasant view out a window, or painting or other artwork.

The dining room is an exception to the feng shui guideline of aiming to leave some open space in the center of every room. Here the dining table itself should occupy the center position, with equal space on all sides (if possible), and plenty of room for each person to sit down at and get up from the table.

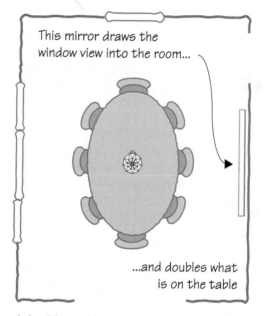

This mirror draws the window view into the room...

...and doubles what is on the table

A chandelier and large mirror enhance the chi of the dining room.

A mirror that reflects what's on the table visually doubles your food, and symbolically doubles your money. Keep in mind, though, that if your dining table is covered with clutter or unfinished projects the mirror will also double the mess and workload.

If your family is managing to dine together (whether in the dining room or elsewhere), but the conversations tend to focus on the past rather than sharing current issues, try clearing all old objects from the dining room or dining area. Boxes of old papers and photographs especially will contribute to holding the energy of this room in the past. Getting rid of them will encourage your family members to open up about what's happening in their lives right now. If you want to keep a few ancestral treasures or portraits in the dining room, place them together in the Family sector of the room rather than distributing them throughout the space.

Eating in Peace

The dining room should be a calm and peaceful place. Warm, soothing earth tones such as soft yellow, peach, and beige are good colors for this room. Curtains soften the cutting chi of mini-blinds, and a thick rug or carpet adds a soothing texture that helps to absorb sound and keeps the atmosphere of this room tranquil.

If you don't have a formal dining room, do what you can to make the area where you have your meals as separate and quiet as possible.

> **It's Elemental** _____
>
> Lighting is an important element in creating a good dining atmosphere. Use candles, lower wattage bulbs, or a dimmer switch to bring the energy level down a little, especially at the end of a hectic day.

If your evening meals often feel rushed or if time pressures from the day carry over into the dinner hour, try removing all clocks and calendars from the dining room and reposition those in other rooms so they can't be seen from the table. This will help you slow down and enjoy a calmer dining experience.

At least once a week turn off the TV and allow yourself to enjoy the process of physical nourishment without any distractions other than conversation with your family. Good manners dictate turning your cell phone off when you dine at a restaurant; why not apply this rule at home, too? Treating the dinner hour as a special time for relaxation and nurturing is a good feng shui practice, and will help both your mood and your digestion.

The Feng Shui Table

Oval dining tables are preferred in feng shui, because the rounded shape helps chi flow through the room more smoothly. When the table is not in use, keep three or more chairs in place at the table. If you want to attract new friends or guests to your home, having at least one more chair at the dining table than there are people in your household will create energetic space to expand your circle of friends.

The head of the household should always sit in the Command Position, at the end of the table farthest from the main door or entrance to the room. When this important seat is empty, or if it is usually occupied by a child, parental authority in the family can be subtly undermined.

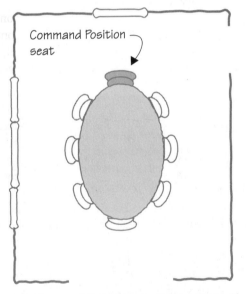

Command Position seat

The Command Position at the dining table should be occupied by the head of the household.

For those who usually dine alone, sitting in a different seat every few nights will help to keep the energy around the table balanced. If you are single and looking for a partner, set the table for two every night, add pinks to your dining room color scheme, and arrange candles, artwork, and other objects around the room in pairs to support romantic connections. When you do invite that special someone over for dinner, sit on adjacent sides of the table, rather than across from each other, to encourage friendly conversation.

> ### Sha Alert!
>
> If anyone in your family is in poor health, make sure he or she is not exposed to any sha chi while dining.

Common causes of sha chi in the dining room include all the usual suspects: ceiling fans, exposed beams, secret arrows from sharp angles or corners, or chi coming through a doorway and hitting the back of a chair.

Many dining rooms are entered through an open archway, where there is no physical door that can be closed. An open door situation such as this can be cured by hanging one or more faceted crystals in the doorway, or by placing a folding screen in front of it during mealtimes.

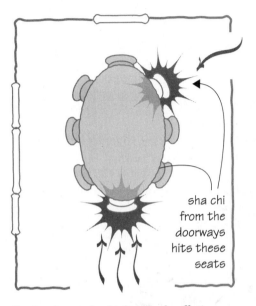

sha chi
from the
doorways
hits these
seats

*Be alert for any sha chi that may be affecting
certain seats in your dining room.*

Savor the Finer Things in Life

Your beautiful table linens and good silverware should
be used from time to time, so you can enjoy their good
chi in the present instead of always saving it for some
future date. Plan a special sit-down-together dinner
with your partner or family one night a month (or
more often, if you can). Making this a regular event
reinforces how special your loved ones are to you.
You can even invite a different family member to have
the Command Position seat during each special dinner, and allow that person to choose the menu for
the night.

It's Elemental

Use a tablecloth, rather than individual placemats, to encourage closeness among family members.

As you set the table for your family dinner, check to make sure you have included objects and/or colors that represent all five of the feng shui elements. When all the elements are brought together in one place, they create balance and harmony throughout the room. Some items you could use include …

- Metal: flatware, silver candlesticks.
- Water: in drinking glasses, a pitcher, or a vase of flowers; blue tablecloth, napkins, or dinnerware.
- Wood: fresh flowers; green tablecloth or napkins.
- Fire: candles; red tablecloth, napkins, or dinnerware; red flowers.
- Earth: porcelain plates; ceramic vase; yellow tablecloth, napkins, or dinnerware.

Take a moment before beginning the meal to give thanks for the abundance on your table and for the family and friends who are sharing it with you. Saying grace before the meal—in whatever form you choose—fills the dining room with the positive chi of love and appreciation.

The Least You Need to Know

- A crystal chandelier or faceted crystal ball over the dining table balances the chi of the room and encourages healthy eating habits.

- Choose colors and imagery to create a peaceful atmosphere in the dining room.

- Clocks and calendars in the dining room can create a feeling of being rushed or stressed during meals.

- Choose a seating arrangement that supports parental authority and encourages peaceful communication.

- Avoid eating in a position where you will be exposed to sha chi.

Chapter 10

Gathering Places

In This Chapter

- Feng shui tips for living rooms and family rooms
- Strengthening family connections
- Sha chi in family spaces, and what to do about it

Your living room, family room, and den are places where you connect with your spouse and children, entertain guests, and relax with friends. The layout and decor of these spaces can support and encourage harmonious family and group relationships or—if there are feng shui problems here—lead to discord and poor communication.

In this chapter, we explore what makes a good (or not so good) environment for these areas of the home, and how you can improve the energy of these rooms to support the family and social relationships that you desire.

Chi Flow for the Living Room

The biggest challenge in the living room is usually how to best arrange the furniture to encourage a good flow of chi. This room needs to be calm enough to relax in, but not so peaceful that you fall asleep on the couch as soon as you sit down after dinner. Major pieces of furniture should be placed so that chi flows gently through the seating areas, rather than leaving them totally becalmed or bombarding a particular spot with too much energy. Too much furniture in too small a space is a common cause of blocked chi.

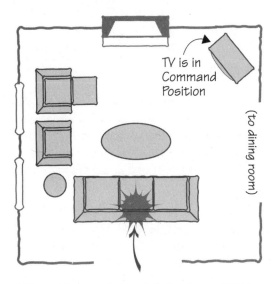

This couch has a good view of the fireplace and TV, but it blocks chi flow into the room.

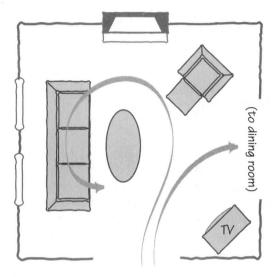

Good chi flow in the living room supports relaxation and communication.

All sitting areas in the living room should be protected from any sources of sha chi. Here are some
situations to avoid if possible, and suggestions for
what to do if they can't be avoided:

- Problem: Sofa placed with its back to the
  door or entrance

  Solutions: Place a table behind the sofa,
  with a lamp or vase of flowers on it; hang
  a faceted crystal between the door and
  the sofa; place a soft-textured rug between
  the door and the sofa.

- Problem: Exposed beam over the sofa or
  other seating area

Solutions: Move the sofa; use the feng shui cures for exposed beams discussed in Chapter 7.

- Problem: Ceiling fan over the sofa or other seating area

  Solution: Hang a faceted crystal ball from the pull-chain.

- Problem: Seating area on the low side of a slanted ceiling

  Solutions: Use this space for a sideboard, table, entertainment center, or bookcase; move seating to the side of the room below the higher ceiling.

- Problem: Secret arrows aimed at a seating area

  Solutions: Reposition seating if possible; use plants or curtains to soften sharp corners; hang a faceted crystal ball between the source of the secret arrows and the seating area.

See Chapter 7 for more information about sources of and solutions to sha chi and secret arrows.

 Sha Alert!

A ceiling fan or exposed beam over a seating area can increase stress, anxiety, depression, or headaches for whoever sits directly underneath it.

Place the most prominent seating—usually the sofa—in the Command Position (on the far side of the room from the door, with a good view of the space and, if possible, a solid wall behind for support). If a single chair in the Command Position is always used by the same person, he or she could dominate family interactions. In many homes, the Command Position is occupied by the television; no wonder we are a nation of couch potatoes!

If you've placed the furniture as best you can for the layout of the room, but the energy still feels chaotic, or people just don't seem to settle down, a gently moving mobile in the Family area of the room can have a soothing effect on the space.

If the energy is too low, use a wind chime in the Family area instead, to energize the space. Choose cooler colors (pale greens, blues, and lavenders) to calm a space down, warmer tones (reds, oranges, bright yellows) to liven things up.

Family Connections

Sitting areas have a strong influence on how people using the space interact with each other. Division within the family may be reflected in the furniture arrangement here; if Dad's lounger is on the far side of the room from where Mom sits on the couch, there's likely to be distance in their relationship as well.

An easy way to strengthen communication is to move living room seating closer together. A shared side table, reading lamp, or coffee table can function as common ground to connect the separate seats around it. To encourage connection between individuals, place groups of smaller objects together on a table within the seating area. For example:

- Three pillar candles together on one plate
- A bowl of polished river stones on the coffee table
- A group of family photographs on a side table (make sure everyone in the family is included!)

 It's Elemental

A single chair in the Marriage area of the living room discourages romantic connections. Add a second, matching chair beside it—or replace it with a love seat—if you want to attract or reignite a romance.

Is there a certain seat in the living room that no one ever uses? Sit in that chair yourself for a few minutes, and try to get a sense of why you prefer to sit elsewhere. If the chair itself is not comfortable, consider getting rid of it. If it's not comfy, it doesn't have good feng shui.

Picture Perfect

The living room is one of the best rooms in the house for imagery that reflects your future goals and ambitions. Anything with a strong personal meaning can be far more powerful than traditional feng shui cures, so go ahead and be creative. (If you want to add some traditional feng shui cures, please see Appendix A for ideas.)

Pay special attention to objects and imagery in these three parts of the room:

- The focal point that first draws your attention as you enter the room
- The area in most prominent view when you sit in your usual seat
- The Fame area (center of rear wall); this is a great place for an image that represents your future ambitions

If what you see in these areas does not reflect what you want from life, replace it with something more in line with your desires. Also check for anything that could be symbolic of conflict or discord of any kind. A room full of happy, friendly imagery will help support a happy, friendly family life. Anything that is less than uplifting does not contribute to a positive atmosphere, especially in the living room; if you can't remove it to another part of the home, place it somewhere out of sight.

Feng Shui and Your Family Photos

Living rooms filled with mementos and old family photographs encourage focusing on the past at the expense of the present and future. For an elderly or retired couple, this may be appropriate. A younger household will benefit from selecting a few special items to display together in the Family area, and moving other treasures worth keeping into storage.

To help bring your extended family closer together, use your living room more often and make sure that the photos you have on display include absent relatives and loved ones and reflect fun times you have had together. Remove photos from times when people were angry or upset, even if those emotions don't show up in the pictures.

When two family members are not getting along, check to see what's going on with the pictures of them on display in the house. In your group photos, is one person always in front of the other, or are they looking in opposite directions? Check the relationship between individual pictures, too. Moving their images farther apart can create space to cool down, if that's what's most needed right now. If distance is a problem, physically bringing pictures closer together helps bring the people in them closer, too.

The Least You Need to Know

- Arrange seating to make it easy for people to connect and converse with each other.
- Use feng shui cures if there is sha chi aimed at the living room couch.
- Living room imagery should reflect your future ambitions.
- How you display your family photos can affect how family members get along.

Chapter

11

In the Bedroom

In This Chapter

- How feng shui can help you get a good night's sleep
- Taking a close look at what's in your bedroom
- Feng shui tips for children's bedrooms
- Easy ways to encourage romance or attract a new relationship

Your bedroom is a key area in the home for applying feng shui cures and enhancements. You spend one third of your time there (or would if you were getting the recommended eight full hours of sleep every night), so this part of the home has a very strong influence on your personal chi and life experiences.

According to the law of proximity, the closer something is to you, the stronger its effects on your energy will be; the bed you sleep in—and any feng shui problems with or around it—will have a powerful effect on your rest, health, and romantic relationships.

The Feng Shui of Your Bed

Feng shui problems in, under, or around your bed can undermine your health, damage your relationships, and make it hard to get the restful sleep you need. When your bed has good feng shui, it helps all aspects of your life go more smoothly.

Feng Fact

Modern feng shui advises that positioning your bed for the best placement within the layout of your room is of much greater importance than what sector of the home your bedroom occupies or what direction your head is in when you lie in bed at night.

In deciding which feng shui changes to make to your bedroom, give good bed placement top priority. Once the bed is in the best position, look for other improvements that can be made and for negative influences against which you should be protected.

Bed Placement

The ideal bed placement is in the Command Position within the bedroom, with equal space on either side of the bed, and where there is a solid wall behind the headboard and no sources of sha chi nearby or overhead. A good view of the door from the bed creates a sense of security and control, which will help you to sleep better.

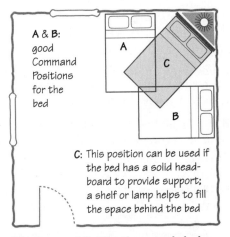

A & B: good Command Positions for the bed

C: This position can be used if the bed has a solid head-board to provide support; a shelf or lamp helps to fill the space behind the bed

The Command Position places your bed where you have a good line of sight to the door but are not directly in line with it.

You might think placing the bed directly across from the door would give you the most command-ing view, but this is called the *Coffin Position* and it should be avoided.

Say "Chi"

In China, the dead are carried from a room feet first. In your bedroom the **Coffin Position** is where the foot of the bed is directly in line with the bedroom door. Sleeping in this position can increase stress and is thought to be very damaging to your health.

It is also important to position the bed so that the side of the bed is not directly exposed to chi coming in the door, as this can cause health problems in the exposed part of the body. In a shared bed, the person who sleeps on the side close to the door will be more strongly affected.

A solid wall behind the head of the bed provides protection and support. If placing your bed under a window is unavoidable, make sure you have a solid, secure headboard, hang a faceted crystal in the window, or place a guardian image in the room so that it can watch over you while you sleep.

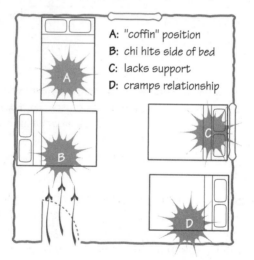

A: "coffin" position
B: chi hits side of bed
C: lacks support
D: cramps relationship

Try not to place your bed in any of these positions.

Those who are in a romantic relationship, or hoping to attract one, should not place the bed so that

one side is much closer to a wall than the other
(see position "D" in the diagram). In a partnership,
the person who sleeps on the open side will have
greater control and freedom, and may even leave
the relationship. For a single person, this position
blocks access by a future partner. If the size or
layout of your bedroom does not allow for equal
space on both sides of the bed, try to allow at least
18 inches between the bed and the side wall.

Sha Alert!

Exposed beams, ceiling fans, skylights,
and slanted ceilings are all sources of sha
chi; don't place your bed under any of
these features if you can possibly avoid it.

If placing your bed in the Command Position will
put it directly under an exposed beam, ceiling fan,
or on the lower side of a slanted ceiling, choose
a different location instead, and use a mirror to
provide a view of the bedroom doorway when you
are lying in bed.

One more consideration in choosing where to place
your bed is to look at what's on the other side of the
wall behind your headboard. A stove, toilet, or fuse
box in this position in the adjoining room can be
very harmful to your health.

There's no need to despair if your bedroom provides only one possible bed position, or if the layout of your room creates problems in every possible

location for the bed. Feng shui is about making the best choices from the options available to you. If there is no good bed position available, place your bed where you feel most comfortable sleeping, and use these feng shui cures to correct or protect against sha chi:

- Problem: The bed is exposed to chi from the doorway.

  Solutions: Hang a faceted crystal ball halfway between the bed and the door; for a bed in the coffin position, place a blanket chest or other low piece of furniture at the foot of the bed to act as a buffer.

- Problem: Exposed beam over the bed.

  Solutions: Hang three, six, or nine faceted crystal balls from the bottom of the beam; hang angel figurines or images on the beam under the beam; use Chinese bamboo flutes as described in Chapter 7 and Appendix A.

- Problem: Bed is directly under a ceiling fan or skylight.

  Solution: Hang a faceted crystal ball over the bed.

- Problem: Bed is on the low side of a room with a slanted ceiling.

  Solutions: Use fabric to create a canopy over the bed; place uplights and/or house plants against the wall; hang two bamboo flutes angled toward each other on the wall above the head of the bed.

- Problem: A source of sha chi on the other side of the wall behind the head of the bed.

  Solutions: Use water element colors and imagery to control the fire energy of a stove or other electrical appliance; use wood element colors and imagery to absorb and lift the draining water energy of a toilet or other plumbing fixture; hang a mirror on the opposite side of the bedroom so it will reflect the bed away from the shared wall, but where you won't see yourself in the mirror when you are lying in bed.

Bed Design

A solid headboard provides support and protection for the sleeper, and is helpful if your bed is not in a strong position within the room. A footboard can also provide protection for the foot of the bed, but if it is very high or you are quite tall it may feel confining; use your own judgment about the effect it is having. Bed designs that feature vertical wooden slats or metal bars can also feel imprisoning; choose a solid headboard design, or make sure you have lots of room on either side of the bed to provide freedom of movement.

Any kind of physical instability around your bed can lead to instability in other areas of life as well. A headboard that is not securely affixed to the bed could affect your health, relationship, and finances, and should be tightened immediately. If your bed frame rolls around a little too easily on its casters, or wobbles in any way, securing it more firmly in place will bring additional stability to all the hours of your day.

Chi should circulate around and under the bed. Platform beds with closed sides—especially those with built-in drawers that slide in and out—are particularly problematic. Not only is it impossible for chi to circulate freely beneath the bed, the contents of and motion of the drawers can also disturb your sleep.

It's Elemental

If you are trying to get pregnant, sleep on a bed that is raised off the floor so chi can circulate underneath it. Don't store anything under the bed, and don't sweep or vacuum under there until your baby is born in order not to disturb the conception and gestation processes.

The mattress of a king-size bed rests on two separate box springs. This hidden division down the center of the bed implies a split in the relationship; it can contribute to conflicts and separation and may even lead to divorce. To cure this split, remove the mattress and place a long piece of red fabric over the line where the two sides of the box spring come together. The fabric should be solid red, at least 36 inches wide, and long enough to wrap around the ends of the box spring and be tucked underneath.

Replace the mattress, knowing that energetically you and your partner can now sleep more closely together.

Futon couches and sleeper sofas are fine for short-term guests but are not appropriate for long-term use. They are usually located in the living room, home office, den, or another location not conducive to rest, and the daily folding and unfolding of the bed and its mixed purpose (couch by day, bed by night) all add up to a poor night's sleep in feng shui terms.

Precious Rest

Bedrooms should be calm spaces for rest and relaxation. If you are not sleeping as well as you'd like to, look around your bedroom with feng shui eyes. Remove sources of unsettled energy, protect yourself from sha chi; and choose colors and imagery that have a soothing (rather than stimulating) effect.

What's in Your Bedroom?

In the fairy tale of the princess and the pea, the princess is invited to sleep on a pile of 20 mattresses with a single pea hidden beneath them. When she complains the next morning of disturbed sleep due to a tiny lump in the mattress, the princess's prospective in-laws know that she is a worthy mate for their son. Modern women are a little tougher than that, and are more likely to be judged on their accomplishments than on their delicacy, but both they and their partners can suffer from feng shui distractions that prevent them from getting a good night's rest.

It's Elemental

Comfort is a sign of good feng shui, so if your mattress is not comfortable it's time to get a new one that will provide the support or cushioning you need. Invest in the best-quality mattress and bedding that you can afford. Better quality means better comfort, and more comfort means better sleep.

If you have recently divorced or separated from a partner, buy a new mattress if you can afford it; the old one will have absorbed a lot of chi from the past relationship. Pillows, sheets, and blankets should all be adequate and comfortable as well, and replaced (if possible) as relationship changes dictate. Don't economize by using second-hand bedding; it could have soaked up all kinds of negative energy from the previous users, and you don't want to be sleeping in that kind of nasty chi every night.

Anything stored underneath your bed will affect you while you sleep. It's best to keep the under-bed area completely open (a decorative bed-skirt is okay); if you have no choice but to use this space for storage, be thoughtful about what you keep there. Extra blankets and towels or soft clothing such as sweaters are comfortable to sleep above. Other items are inappropriate for under-bed storage:

- Books, magazines, and work or school papers can be intellectually stimulating at night when you want to turn your brain off for a while and go to sleep.

- Shoes, sneakers, workout clothes, or sports equipment can keep you pacing the floor or running around all night, either literally or in your dreams.

- Weapons of any kind and sharp or metal objects symbolize cutting or stabbing energy that can damage your health or lead to accidents or robberies.

- Clothing, objects, or photographs from past relationships or a difficult period of your life can hinder your current happiness and future progress.

Everything in the bedroom will affect you strongly in feng shui terms. Your bed and the items closest to it are critical, but everything else in the room is important as well. Look at every object in your bedroom with an eye to its symbolic meaning. Three things that are frequently found in bedrooms—but don't belong there—are desks, exercise equipment, and the television.

Any kind of desk or workspace brings inappropriate energy of intellectual activity into the bedroom. No matter how tired you are physically, this energy can be mentally over-stimulating and interfere with your sleep. And since good feng shui dictates that both the bed and the desk be in the Command Position, when they are in the same room it's likely that one or both key pieces of furniture is in an inauspicious location. If you have a desk in your bedroom, shield your view of it from the bed with a folding screen or curtain.

Exercise equipment is also disruptive in the bedroom, even if it's been buried under a pile of laundry for months. Subconsciously, it will remind you of working out when you should be sleeping, and exercise equipment that's been gathering dust for months can trigger feelings of guilt about not taking better care of your body.

 Sha Alert! _____

A stationary bicycle, rowing machine, or stair-climber in the bedroom can indicate that your romantic relationships require a lot of effort but never go anywhere.

Televisions are also disruptive in the bedroom, especially if you are in the habit of watching from bed just before going to sleep at night. Distressing news reports and late-night comedy shows are equally capable of affecting your energy long after you've turned the TV off. If you feel you just have to have a television in the bedroom, keep it in an armoire or cabinet with doors you can close, or cover it with a shawl or attractive piece of fabric at night.

Make sure that the first thing you see when you enter the bedroom, and whatever you are looking at when you lie or sit in bed, are peaceful and relaxing images. The area directly across from the bed is a good place to hang imagery or a collage representing the things and experiences you want to attract into your life.

Children's Bedrooms

Bedrooms should be places of relaxation for children, too. The bold primary colors, busy wallpaper, and clutter of toys, books, and games that fill many children's rooms create a stimulating environment that is not appropriate for a bedroom. Use feng shui principles to create a more soothing environment for your little ones, especially if they often have trouble calming down and going to sleep at night:

- Choose pastel colors over primary shades.

- Use toy chests and storage containers to keep the chaos under control.

- Keep the space under the bed open; don't use it for storage if you can avoid it.

- Place the bed in the Command Position; for a young child, placing one side of the bed against a wall can provide additional support during the growing years.

- Move sports trophies away from the area around the bed; remove action figures from the bed area also, unless they are providing your child with a feeling of security and protection.

Teens are at an age of discovery, and their need to assert independence should be honored. Let them do what they want with their own spaces (within reasonable limits, of course). If your teen shows an interest in feng shui, that's great; offer your support, but don't insist on making specific changes. It is never appropriate to use feng shui in someone else's space without his or her permission.

Turning Up the Heat

Your bedroom is the best place for feng shui enhancements to support romance and marriage, regardless of what sector of the ba gua it is in. Decorate the room with colors, objects, and imagery that reflect your ideal relationship and encourage romance.

Pinks and pale greens are good colors for the bedroom, as are warm shades of white and ivory. Red is an excellent accent color to inspire increased passion and intensity. Floral artwork, wallpaper, draperies, and rugs, especially with lots of pink or green, are also good in the bedroom. Clean lines, spare décor, and earth-tone colors are just as appropriate for those who prefer simpler décor; small feng shui accents such as a pink faceted crystal hung over the bed, a figurine of a couple embracing, or two pink roses in a crystal vase stand out even more clearly against a neutral background.

In addition to equal space on both sides of the bed (to encourage equality in your relationship), you should have two nightstands that are a matched pair or similar in size. A single nightstand implies that the room is used by a single person, so set the room up for a couple if you want to be part of one. A single person who wants to attract a relationship should also sleep in a double or queen-sized bed; single beds are for children and single adults, not for couples. Instead of sprawling across the whole bed, sleep on the same side every night, with the intention that your perfect partner will soon be sleeping on the other side next to you.

One simple and very powerful way to encourage the appearance of new romantic partner in your life is to literally make space for that person. In addition to sleeping on one side of a couple-sized bed, clean out at least 25 percent of the space in your bedroom closet, dresser drawers, and bookshelves. Make space as well in other places a partner might wish to keep some of his or her things throughout the home: the bathroom cabinet, the refrigerator, and the media rack in the living room, to name a few examples.

The Marriage area within the bedroom—the far right corner of the room from the doorway—deserves special attention if you want to attract a new relationship or heat up your love life. Remove all clutter from this area, and decorate it with imagery that symbolizes love and partnership. Include some fire energy, such as two heart-shaped red accent pillows, two red candles, or even a string of novelty lights shaped like hot peppers.

It's Elemental

Romantic relationships are all about pairing up, so placing lots of things in pairs in your bedroom—and in all the Marriage areas throughout your house—will strengthen your current relationship and help attract a new partner if you are single.

Whether you are yearning for someone with whom to share your heart and home, or just craving a good night's sleep, improving the feng shui of your bedroom will help you achieve greater happiness and fulfillment in all aspects of your life.

The Least You Need to Know

- Placing your bed in the Command Position will help you get a good night's sleep.

- Under-bed storage space should be used only for soft, comfortable items such as extra bedding.

- Sha chi around your bed can cause or aggravate health problems and damage your relationship.

- The Marriage area in your bedroom is the best place for feng shui enhancements to attract or encourage romance.

Feng Shui for the Home Office

In This Chapter

- Choosing the best location for your home office
- Feng shui tips for office furnishings
- Creating good chi for your work space

More and more people are working from home now, either part- or full-time, and many of them don't have a really good place for a home office. While more and more contemporary home designs incorporate spaces that can be used for an office, many older or smaller homes or apartments present quite a challenge. And because a home office, by definition, brings the energy of work and business into the home, this creates its own confusion. In this chapter, we take a look at some essential feng shui factors to keep in mind when setting up—or relocating—your home office.

Location, Location, Location

Many home offices are set up in whatever space is available: a corner of the bedroom, on the dining room table, down in the basement or upstairs in the attic, or in the guest bedroom. Some of these locations are fine places for a home office; others are not so great. Here are some guidelines to keep in mind when deciding where to set up your in-home workspace.

It's Elemental

The basic feng shui guidelines you've learned in this book—creating a good flow of chi, using the Command Position, protecting yourself from sha chi, and dealing with clutter—are just as important in an office location as they are at home.

There are essentially two kinds of home offices: home administration centers that are used for paying household bills, keeping track of the family budget, and other household management tasks; and work spaces related to earning an income that are located within the home. For home administration, a corner of the kitchen counter may be sufficient. If you are working from home professionally—even if it's just part time—it is best to have a space that is used only for that purpose in order to keep work and home energies as separate at possible.

If you hold client meetings in your home office, it is best if clients can use a separate entrance from that used by your family. That way your clients can come and go without having to pass through your living spaces, and both of your energies will remain focused on business. Clients who walk through your living space before getting to the office are likely to make a subtle shift away from a business focus, and their confidence in your professionalism or capabilities may subconsciously be weakened.

back door is office entry

home office

front door

The ideal home office is as separate as possible from the rest of the house.

Make sure there is a clear pathway to your home business entrance, especially if it is at the side or back of the house, so your clients know which way to go when they arrive for the first time. Because office and home functions are different, your home office has its own Mouth of Chi, whether that's a separate exterior door or a door inside the home. All of the guidelines for good doorway chi presented in Chapter 5 will be equally important for your home office.

Home Office Locations and the Ba Gua

You can use the ba gua for your house to help choose a good location for your home office, depending on the type of work that you do:

- Office in the Career area: good for writing, publishing, anything related to communication or that brings people together
- Office in the Knowledge area: good for tutoring, counseling services
- Office in the Family area: good for family counseling, network marketing, wellness services
- Office in the Wealth area: good for financial planning, charitable organizations
- Office in the Fame area: good for public relations, marketing
- Office in the Marriage area: good for dating and wedding services, marriage counseling, wellness services

- Office in the Children & Creativity area: good for anything child-related, teaching and tutoring, creative writing, art, graphic design

- Office in the Mentors & Travel area: good for personal coaching, counseling, travel-related services

Attics are associated with future aspirations in feng shui; this could be a good home office location for someone involved in strategic planning or for a personal coach. And basements are associated with the subconscious and underlying issues that have their roots in past experiences, which could be a good location for a therapist. (Attics and basements do have some specific problems that you'll want to watch out for, however, so be sure to read the comments in the next section if you are considering a home office in either of these spaces.)

Remember that the best feng shui decisions are often a matter of making trade-offs. The appropriate ba gua area for your career may not be the best choice for your home office if that space does not have good feng shui in other ways. Be sure to consider accessibility, lighting, and room layout as well. Wherever your office is located, do find the relevant career-related area of the ba gua within the room, and make sure that is decorated with appropriate colors, objects, and imagery.

Where Not to Work

Certain areas of the home are especially ill-suited for home office use. Here are some locations that you should avoid if at all possible:

- Location: Center of the home (Tai Chi)

  Problem: Work will dominate over family life

- Location: Bedroom

  Problems: Work issues may cause or contribute to relationship conflicts; thoughts of work may interfere with sleep; you may feel drowsy and unfocused when trying to work

- Location: Office in nook underneath stairs

  Problems: Oppressive overhead energy may cause headaches, contribute to difficulty concentrating; unevenly shaped space causes energy imbalance; impossible to work in the Command Position

- Location: Next to bathroom, with desk and toilet on opposite sides of the shared wall

  Problem: Business chi gets flushed down the toilet

Some other situations to be alert for are rooms with low or slanted ceilings, and poor lighting or ventilation (all of which may affect an attic room). If your office has a slanted ceiling, place your desk on the taller side of the room, and use the lower side for file cabinets, bookcases, or other storage. Plants and lights that shine upward (rather than down) are good additions to rooms with low or slanted ceilings.

Sha Alert!

A low ceiling in your office can suppress aspirations and keeps you focused on the details of the present rather than exploring future possibilities. Slanted ceilings in the office create a similar problem that is focused on one side of the room.

Basements often offer extra space to create a home office without interfering with the rest of the house. The problem with basements is that they are usually cool and damp, either inadequately lit or with harsh overhead fluorescent fixtures, and they often have poor ventilation. Windows, if there are any, may be small, dirty, and positioned so high on the wall that you can't see out of them—not good for having a clear vision of your future direction.

Don't despair if it seems that none of your home office options are any good. Feng shui is about doing the best you can with the space you have. If you must work in the bedroom, for example, you can set up the office in an armoire-type unit and close it up when it is not in use. A folding screen or a fabric curtain can also help to keep work and home energies separate. And if your office space has design features that are less than ideal, feng shui cures such as bells, crystals, and mirrors can help to correct them. You'll find lots of good ideas throughout this book, or refer to the feng shui cures in Appendix A.

Seats of Power

The furnishings you choose for your home office—especially your desk and chair—can have a powerful influence on your ability to succeed and prosper. When setting up a home office, it can be tempting to use whatever extra furniture is on hand around the house or to economize with second-hand furnishings. Neither of these is a very good idea.

Ergonomics—how well the shape, size, and other design features of your desk, chair, and lighting work for you—is a very important consideration for any work space. Sure, using that extra kitchen chair is a lot cheaper than buying a new "executive-style" office chair, but if it's not comfortable it is not helping you get your work done. A lamp that's fine on a bedside table in the bedroom may be woefully inadequate as task lighting for your workspace.

 It's Elemental

> If you are going to work from home, make sure your home office is working for you by investing in comfortable furnishings that make it easy to focus on business.

Second-hand office furniture requires special consideration, as it often has terrible "predecessor chi." Never buy used furniture from a business that went bankrupt, no matter how cheap it is—it will fill your home office with the energy of failure, anxiety, and disappointment. On the other hand, if you absolutely positively know for sure that the previous user of your second-hand desk chair made a zillion dollars in a legal and ethical manner and is now living a life of ease in Acapulco, go ahead and take it! All those good success vibes will help you prosper as well.

Family furniture hand-me-downs will have good or bad energy for you depending on the quality of your family relationships. If you have a great relationship with your dad, for example, and consider him a good role model, using his old desk and chair in your office can help you feel looked after, supported, and inspired.

In general, a large desk provides energetic room for expansive thinking and growth. However, too much large furniture in a too-small room will stop chi cold, and you may discover that there's no new business coming in.

Sha Alert!

> If you sit at your desk with your back to the door, or don't have a clear view of door, you are not in the Command Position. This can mean that you are not in control of what's going on in your business, and that new developments (and problems!) often take you by surprise.

If you can't place your desk in the Command Position (facing the door, but not directly across from it, and with a solid wall behind you for support), use a mirror to provide a reflected view of the doorway. And keep in mind that a desk in the Command Position is only helpful if you are able to get in and out of your chair with ease, otherwise you may feel "backed up against the wall" by business situations.

A good desk chair can be adjusted to the correct height for your body and work surface, is stable, and provides good back and arm support. Your desk chair represents your support and foundation, so make sure it is in good shape for the job.

If you are buying a new chair, think about what colors (based on the five elements and the ba gua) would be good for both your office location and your type of business. For example, communication is associated with water and the Career area, so a dark blue or black chair would be an appropriate choice for a writer, publisher, or other communications-related career. Since water is created by metal, gray would also be a supportive color choice. However, brown or burgundy would not be good for a writer, because earth and fire weaken water.

If your chair is not a supportive color for your profession, a very easy solution is to cover it with a piece of fabric of a more appropriate color.

Remember that the work you do is a form of self-expression. Although it is important that your office furniture be ergonomically suited to the work you do, don't feel you have to give this space an "office" look unless it helps you concentrate on business.

The View from the Top

In the corporate world, successful entrepreneurs are often described as being "visionaries," in reference to their ability to conceive and implement dramatically new ideas that transform entire industries. In feng shui, "vision"—both physical eyesight and imaginative power—is symbolically associated with the Fame gua, with lighting of any kind, and with the windows in your home or office.

An office that lacks windows—such as a home office stuffed into a corner of the basement—keeps you out of sight of others and can lead to feeling isolated and out of touch. If you are working at home for someone else, you could be "out of the loop" with what's going on in the rest of the company. For an entrepreneur working from home, a windowless office implies you could be out of touch with your clients and that you are unable to foresee where your entire industry is headed.

 It's Elemental

In feng shui terms, dirty windows mean cloudy or muddled thinking, contribute to a negative outlook on life, and may limit your work prospects. If you're feeling a need for clarity or could use a brighter outlook on the future, grab a roll of paper towels and bottle of window cleaner and get those windows sparkly clean!

If your office has small, high windows or no view at all, use posters of landscapes with a far horizon to create the illusion of being able to see into the distance. Since windows also help chi to circulate, you may need to use a fan or mobile to help move chi around.

It's also important to pay attention to what you see outside your office windows. If there are any secret arrows aimed your way, keep the blinds closed (it's best if you can use material that will allow light in while blocking an unattractive view).

If you are fortunate in having a beautiful, inspiring view outside your office windows, a large wall mirror can reflect the view into the room and fill the room with positive chi. But note that mirrors can be tricky in a home office. A mirror that reflects your desk can symbolically double your work. In terms of your income, this could be good. But how well will you handle the increased workload? Sometimes more work means more stress, contributes to family problems, and leads to physical or emotional exhaustion. And unless you keep your desk very tidy, that mirror will be doubling your mess and clutter as well!

Good lighting is essential in any office. In addition to helping you get your work done without eyestrain, bright lights in feng shui terms also support business success. Fluorescent lights are generally awful and should be avoided if at all possible. If you must work under fluorescent lights, get outside for at least 15 to 20 minutes a day during your lunch break or after work, and wash your face and hands several times a day to help refresh your energy.

The things that you see within your office are important as well. Here are some factors that may merit attention:

- Keep all clocks and calendars in the office set or turned to the correct date and time, or you may find yourself seriously out of synch with the needs of your business.

- A clock directly in your line of sight as you work at your desk, or on the wall above your desk, can contribute to feeling time pressure. Move your office clock so it is in a place where you can check the time if you need to, but where it is not ticking away right in front of you.

- Do not place unpaid bills where you will see them first thing when you enter the office or when you sit down at your desk. They will keep your attention focused on expenses, rather than on income.

- If you face the wall when seated at your desk, be sure to decorate the space directly in front of you in some way. Facing a blank wall implies a blank state of mind, and can contribute to feeling blocked or frustrated. Make sure that you are looking at something inspiring: a photograph of your spouse and/or kids, a brochure for that exotic vacation you hope to take by the end of the year, a mock-up of the "Entrepreneur of the Year" award you hope to win someday, or any kind of artwork that inspires you.

In general, all of the imagery in your office should be as positive and prosperous-looking as possible. Anything indicating poverty or lack does not belong here.

Clutter in your home office is just as bad as in the rest of the house. Clutter is distracting, makes it hard to focus, and drains your energy. Make a special effort to keep the surface of your desk and the areas immediately around you clutter-free. Hidden clutter counts, too. If you want to bring in more clients and business, go through your paper and digital files and physically create room for the new documents that will accompany expansion of your business.

The Least You Need to Know

- The basics of good feng shui are just as important in your office space as they are in the rest of your home.
- Never use second-hand office furniture from a business that went bankrupt.
- Choose furnishing colors and materials that are an elemental match for your career.
- Office windows, lighting, and imagery can affect your present energy as well as your ability to clearly envision the future of your business.

Hooray for Indoor Plumbing!

In This Chapter

- Why the bathroom has a bad reputation in feng shui
- The worst places for a bathroom (and some not-so-bad ones)
- How to prevent a bathroom from draining chi away from a key area of your home

The bathroom has a bad reputation in feng shui, and in some ways this is deserved, as you will discover. But it's not all negative. Comfort, cleanliness, and convenience are key ingredients to good feng shui, and our modern bathrooms provide them all.

Bathrooms and the Ba Gua

One of the challenges posed by the modern bathroom is that there's no good place for it in the ba gua, which long predates indoor plumbing.

We can look at the ba gua and see at a glance that the Family area would be a good place for the living room, that a home office is well placed in the Knowledge, Wealth, or Career sectors, and that the Marriage corner of the house is a great place for the master bedroom. But where does the bathroom go?

Challenging Bathroom Locations

The bathroom is a little out of place anywhere, although some locations are more troublesome than others. The thing to keep in mind is that bathroom plumbing has a draining effect wherever it is located. You can look at where the bathrooms in your house are according to the ba gua to see which areas are being weakened. For example …

- A bathroom in the Wealth area can drain your finances.
- A bathroom in the Fame area could mean your reputation is "in the toilet."
- In the Marriage area, a bathroom could be flushing your happiness away.
- If you have a bathroom in the Career area, opportunities might seem to flow away before you can benefit from them.

In evaluating the locations of the bathrooms in your house, keep in mind that the water energy associated with the bathroom is appropriate in the Career area, and nurtures the wood energy of the Family and Wealth areas. In these cases, the draining effect of the bathroom plumbing may still be problem, but the elemental match of the water element to that area of the ba gua is supportive. And, since bathrooms are where we do a lot of our self-care and pampering, they relate energetically to the maternal, nurturing qualities of the Marriage gua as well.

The least-damaging places for bathrooms are the areas straddling two different guas; because the draining energy is not concentrated in one area of the ba gua, the negative effects are less strong.

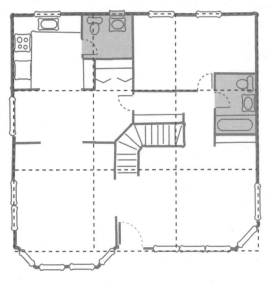

Bathrooms that straddle more than one gua have a weaker negative effect.

A bathroom that is outside the main body of the house is also less of a problem, although it does offset some of the positive benefit of an "extension" of the floor plan.

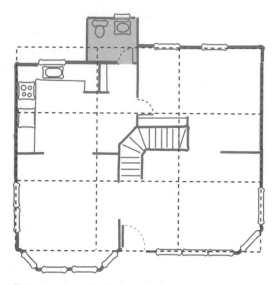

In an extension, the bathroom's draining energy is moved away from the main body of the house.

Some very difficult bathroom locations are next to or above the front door and on the second floor directly above the kitchen.

These locations are particularly difficult because:

- A bathroom in the front hall, close to the door, can drain chi away before it has a chance to circulate through the rest of the house.

- A second-floor bathroom above the front door floods the Mouth of Chi with negative energy.

- The water energy in a bathroom above the kitchen will extinguish the hearth's fire energy, and flood the entire kitchen with negative energy. This is potentially damaging to both health and prosperity.

Sha Alert!

The worst location for a bathroom is in the Tai Chi (the physical center of your home), where it will destabilize the energy of the entire home and weaken every area of the ba gua.

If you suspect that the bathrooms in your house are affecting important guas, there's no need to panic. Use these simple feng shui remedies and the color guidelines that follow to help keep your health, wealth, and happiness from flowing down the drain:

- Problem: bathroom in an important gua (Wealth, Fame, Marriage, etc.) or near the front door

  Solutions: Hang a full-length mirror on the outside of the bathroom door to help deflect chi so it won't be drained away; keep sink and shower drains closed when not in use; keep the toilet seat/lid down when not in use.

- Problem: bathroom in the center of the home

  Solutions: Paint the walls red, and place a stone, large crystal, or other earth-type object (such as a heavy ceramic bowl, vase, or stat-uette) in each corner to help stabilize the energy; a mirror on the outside of the door is highly recommended for this bathroom location.

- Problem: bathroom over the front door or over the kitchen

  Solutions: Hang a faceted crystal in the cen-ter of the bathroom; place a three-inch round mirror on the ceiling directly above the toilet to visually reverse the downward flow of water (use double-sided tape to hold the mirror in place); place earth-type objects in the corners of the bathroom to stabilize the energy; add an image such as a bird or tree to the downstairs area below the bathroom to help lift the energy there.

Bathrooms are places for purification and cleansing, so a sanitary bathroom strengthens and supports this important energy. A dirty bathroom, on the other hand, emphasizes the negative qualities of this room. If your bathroom occupies any of the more challeng-ing locations I've described, it is especially important to keep it sparkling clean, tidy, and well lit.

Color Choices for the Bathroom

This is one of those areas of feng shui where there are two very different schools of thought. Some practitioners believe that strengthening the gua where a bathroom is located will strengthen the neg-ative effect as well. For example, since a bathroom in the Wealth area drains your finances (the thinking goes), adding green and purple colors, which strengthen Wealth, will mean even more money gets washed away. They advise using earth and metal colors and objects to weaken that gua instead, thus (supposedly) weakening the harmful effect.

Other practitioners (myself included) think this is a good example of "throwing the baby out with the bath water." According to the five element cycles, you cannot strengthen (or weaken) one element without having a corresponding effect on the other elements as well. When wood is strengthened, water is weakened; therefore, adding wood-type energy to a bathroom helps bring the strong water element back into balance. Our strategy is to strengthen the affected gua and use the elements to counteract the imbalance of too much water.

Feng Fact

The vastly improved sanitation provided by the modern bathroom means that these rooms are not as threatening to our health and well-being as traditional feng shui teachings might lead us to believe. Not only do our municipal water authorities provide us with an endless supply of clean water, but most of us also bathe regularly and wash our hands several times a day. The kinds of disease and pestilence associated with bathroom functions in ancient times are unlikely to be lurking in the modern American bathroom.

A clean and nicely furnished bathroom deserves to be enjoyed and appreciated in spite of any potentially negative effect. Do what you can to counteract the draining effects of your bathroom's plumbing, then use colors and other décor to balance and support that gua, and you can relax, knowing that you have optimized this challenging area of the home. Here are some guidelines to get you started:

- Bathroom in the Career area: Dark blue and black are usually good colors for the Career area, but there's already so much water in the bathroom that adding more will just increase the imbalance. Choose earth colors instead to stabilize this strong water area.

- Bathroom in the Knowledge area: Reds, browns, and yellows support the earth element associated with this gua and help keep excessive water energy under control. Keep green to a minimum here, as it weakens earth.

- Bathroom in the Family area: This is a good place for that tropical jungle look, with lots of green colors and living plants if there's enough space and light for them. Don't be afraid to go big and bold. For the less adventurous, a serene pastel green will do fine here, too.

- Bathroom in the Wealth area: If you are brave enough to paint your bathroom purple, this is the place to do it. Lavender will do for those who prefer a subtler look, or you can stick with the greens that are also appropriate for this area. Gold accents can be used here to add a look of luxury, but take care not to add too much metal.

- Bathroom in the Fame area: Plants and other wood element objects and colors are especially helpful here because all that wood energy absorbs excess water and nourishes the fire element associated with this gua. Use red, too, either in a big way or as subtle accents. Do make sure to use some wood energy here along with the red; without it you'll be pitting fire against water, never a good idea in feng shui.

- Bathroom in the Marriage area: Beige and pink are the best colors here, and red accents are also good. Pale green shades help bring the water element back into balance, but too much green here will weaken the earth element associated with this gua. Nurturing is a key aspect of this gua, so make this bathroom really comfortable and welcoming.

- Bathroom in the Children & Creativity area: Water here is depleting the metal energy associated with this gua, but adding more metal (white, chrome) will also strengthen water, and we don't want to do that in a bathroom. Instead, use earth colors (browns, beiges) to support metal. A little green is okay here for accents, but too much will weaken metal.

- Bathroom in the Mentors & Travel area: This is another metal area, so the guidelines for the Children & Creativity area apply here as well. Gray is also a good color to use here.

> **It's Elemental** _____
>
> Adding wood energy to a bathroom with living plants, leaf-patterned accessories, and green accent colors will help to absorb excess water chi.

No matter which cures and colors you choose to use, it's important that you are happy with how your bathroom looks and feels. One person might choose natural crystals as earth-type objects to add stability to the bathroom; someone else might prefer to represent earth with a dark brown wicker magazine rack or a ceramic soap dish. One person might love an all-purple bathroom; someone else may be happiest with a few subtle lavender accents. Always be guided by your own personal style and preferences. Remember, if you don't like it, it's not good feng shui, no matter how effective it may be in other ways.

Your Spa of Serenity

After implementing the necessary precautions I've already described, you can further improve the chi of the bathroom by making it as pleasant a space as possible. This is where you begin and end the active part of each day, so the more attractive and inviting you can make it the better.

Most of us live hectic, stressful lives, and are in serious need of soothing places where we can relax and unwind. A clean, tidy, nicely appointed bathroom invites you to soak your worries away in a hot bath with lavender-scented bath salts. Make this pampering experience even nicer with candlelight, soft music, and a pile of fresh fluffy towels with which to dry off. All-white bathroom décor can seem cold and clinical; add warmth with pastel-colored towels and accessories, colorful scented candles, and attractive artwork.

Architects and designers have caught on to our need for a place for self-renewal. *En suite* master baths, where the bathroom area is open to the master bedroom, are very popular these days. The problem with this arrangement is that the bedroom is exposed to the draining energy of the bathroom all night. Poor sleep, low energy, and other health problems can result.

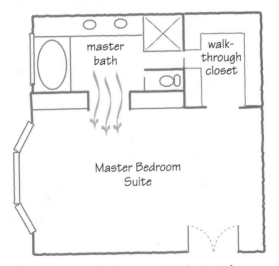

An en suite master bath exposes the bedroom to the bathroom's draining energy.

The best way to cure an en suite bathroom is to install a door to close off the open access. If that's not possible, put up a curtain that can be pulled closed at night, or use one or more faceted crystal balls in the open entry to interrupt chi flowing through the access space.

The Least You Need to Know

- Bathrooms can drain the energy from key areas of your home.

- A mirror on the outside of a bathroom door helps keep chi from draining away.

- Plants and wood-type energy in the bathroom help to absorb excess water chi.

- A door, curtain, or other energy barrier protects a bedroom from the draining energy of an adjoining *en suite* bath.

- Bathrooms aren't all bad; we're definitely better off with than without them, so treat yours like an important part of the home.

Chapter 14

The Secret Life of Housework

In This Chapter

- What you need to know about laundry and other chores
- How minor plumbing leaks and electrical problems could be affecting your finances and health
- Why curb appeal is important, even if you aren't thinking about selling your home

Clean chi is good chi. In every feng shui seminar there comes a moment when the students realize that good housekeeping habits are at least as important—if not more so—than the fun feng shui stuff like bamboo flutes, ba gua mirrors, faceted crystal balls and wind chimes. Feng shui consultants see this in their client's homes as well. Often the most urgent feng shui "cures" involve taking care of overlooked tasks, such as replacing a cracked window, getting piles of to-be-recycled-someday stuff off the front porch, and catching up with basic housework.

Although you might not feel excited about adding housekeeping tasks to your feng shui to-do list, there is a very nice benefit to seeing these chores from a new perspective. When you realize how powerful cleaning up can be as a way to shift the energy of your home environment, you are more likely to make time for it in your busy schedule or to find room for housekeeping help in your budget. If your energy sags at the idea of cleaning up, try consciously focusing on household tasks as caring for your home, with the understanding that by caring for your home you are also caring for yourself and your family. This simple attitude change can turn what used to feel like drudgery into a form of devotion to self and family.

Laundry and Other Chores

Many people have lovely formal entries that they rarely use; all that good energy around the Mouth of Chi is wasted if you pass through a grubby, untidy utility room every day instead of using the front door. Dirty laundry and unwashed dishes—and anything else smelly, unsightly, or unsanitary—sully the energy of the spaces around them.

The kitchen and utility room are two areas of the house where clutter and unwashed things naturally accumulate. If you usually enter and leave your home through these spaces—as many people do, since these rooms often connect the house with the garage—you could be exposed to the sha chi of neglect every time you enter and leave the house.

Sha Alert!

Walking through clutter, grime, and piles of dirty laundry or dishes as you leave the house every morning will rob you of the vitality you need to get through the day. And when it's the first thing you see when you come home at night, it will drag your energy down no matter how many good things happened to you that day.

Learning to Love Laundry

If you are finding it difficult to feel inspired about paying more attention to laundry (not usually at the top of anyone's "Things I Care Deeply About" list), it might help to take a look at what part of the ba gua your laundry is piling up in. Do you really want those grubby towels and smelly socks lingering in your Wealth or Marriage area (for example) any longer than necessary?

Keep in mind that, like bathrooms, laundry rooms have a lot of water energy and a potentially draining effect on the energy of that area. Use your understanding of the interactions of the elements to evaluate whether or not to adjust the color and décor of these spaces to make them more harmonious with their location in the ba gua.

> **It's Elemental**
>
> A utility or laundry room in a key gua is not necessarily a bad thing. Remember that these functions are important and deserve some space in your home. Choose to see the benefit of a clean financial picture, a spotless reputation, or a well-maintained marriage, for example, depending on the gua involved.

Most people don't think about decorating a laundry room, but once you do you'll realize what a big difference a little bit of attention to décor can make here. Small changes are easy and fun, and can have an effect that far exceeds their size. Here are some ideas to get you started, but also use your imagination. The possibilities are endless:

- Laundry room in the Career area: Water is at home here, and the metal-energy color of white appliances is supportive. Chrome and dark blue are good accent colors. Play up the aquatic connection, and don't be afraid to make this space playful and fun, such as with fish-shaped magnets and cabinet knobs. Sometimes we forget that the best jobs are the ones where we feel like we are being paid to play.

- Laundry room in the Knowledge area: Water energy here could get a little wishy-washy, so add earth energy to ground and stabilize this space. Decorate with browns and pale blues, and choose earth-type accents such square decorative tiles in earthy colors to hang on the wall.

- Laundry room in the Family area: Water here supports wood energy. The best colors are pale shades of green and blue. If you've got wall space available, create a gallery of informal family photos here.

- Laundry room in the Wealth area: Use a green or purple laundry basket; organize little things like clothes pins and dryer sheets in a green or purple utility basket; refresh dingy cabinets with a coat of pale green paint.

- Laundry room in the Fame area: Water fights the fire energy associated with Fame, so add lots of wood (green colors, plants) to absorb some of the water and nourish fire. Look for opportunities to add fire energy as well, such as painting all the cabinet knobs and drawer-pulls red.

- Laundry room in the Marriage area: This location will benefit from lots of earth tones and pink accents, especially if you have white (metal energy) appliances. Avoid dark colors here and look for opportunities to group items together in pairs, such as two small utility baskets side by side in the Marriage area of the room.

- Laundry room in the Children & Creativity area: Metal is depleted by water, so keep the décor white and bright. Some splashes of

> color are fine, especially if they come
> from a display of your kids' artwork.

- Laundry room in the Mentors & Travel
  area: This gua is also a metal area, so décor
  here should emphasize white, gray, and
  metallics. Earth-type accent colors and
  accessories are also good.

It's rare to have a laundry room in the Tai Chi
(center) of the house. If you do, be sure to keep
the room clean and bright, and place a full-length
mirror on the outside of the door. Yellow is a good
color here, and you can place a stone or crystal in
each corner of the room for earth element stability.

Wherever your laundry room is located (or wherever your laundry basket is stored, if you don't have
a laundry room), the impact of dirty laundry can be
minimized by keeping it in an attractive hamper or
basket, preferably one with a lid. If you usually wait
until practically all the clothes in the house need
washing before tackling this chore, think about
whether doing less laundry more frequently could
help you keep a tidier home. Putting clean laundry
away after it is done, rather than leaving it in heaps
on that chair in the bedroom for days on end, is
also a good feng shui practice. Unsorted, wrinkled
laundry, even if clean, radiates the energy of unfinished business throughout the house.

Caring for Your Kitchen

As the place where we store and prepare our food,
the state of your kitchen can have a big impact on

your family's health. Dirty dishes in the sink, a smelly garbage can, and stale food in the refrigerator can all affect your family's well-being on an energetic level. Make sure that your kitchen is always clean and tidy, even if that means you won't be able to give quite so much housekeeping attention to the rest of the house.

In an ideal world, every room in your home will always be neat and spotlessly clean. In practical application, however, feng shui is often about doing the best you can with a less-than-ideal situation. If you don't have the time, energy, or domestic help needed to keep the whole house immaculate all the time, put cleaning up the kitchen at the top of your priority list. Use whatever cleanup time and energy you have left over to tackle those areas of the house that correspond to the key issues in your life, based on the ba gua.

Basic Maintenance

Do you and your romantic (or business) partner spend a lot of time and emotional energy dealing with issues from the past that just don't seem to go away? If so, take a look around the Marriage area— which also governs business relationships—of your home or office for anything long-neglected that should be cleaned, dealt with, or thrown out. Be sure to check under your bed and in the Marriage guas of the attic and basement as well.

> ### It's Elemental
>
> If you feel discouraged about your love life, career, finances, or any other aspect of life, go to the corresponding area of the ba gua (indoors and out) and clean everything in sight.

Here are some other specific ways that neglected housekeeping chores or home maintenance issues could be affecting you:

- Leaky plumbing may not seem like such a big deal, until you consider this: In feng shui terms, water flow equals cash flow. Any kind of plumbing leak, whether it's a dripping showerhead or faucet or a hidden leak in the basement, implies that your financial resources are leaking away as well.

- The electrical system in your house is symbolically associated with the nervous system in your body. If anyone in your family is suffering from a nervous system disorder of any kind, make sure that all of your wiring is up to code (for safety reasons, as well as for health), and that any problems with the electrical system—even something as minor as an outlet that doesn't work—are taken care of promptly.

- Dirty windows are hard to see out of, and even a small film of dirt or dust can significantly cut down on the amount of light that passes through them into your home. In feng shui terms, dirty windows can cloud your thinking and affect your vision, either literally in the sense of aggravated vision problems such as cataracts, or symbolically in the sense that you may not be able to "see clearly" what's going on in certain areas of your life.

- Underground spaces are prone to flooding, damp, spiders, mildew, and all sorts of nasty smells and generally yucky chi. When these are present under your house, you may feel that the people, things, and relationships that form the emotional foundation of your life feel a little unstable, unreliable, or just unsavory, even if the stability of your home's physical foundation is unaffected.

- Dirt in the nooks and crannies around your house can be just as harmful, if not as visible, as stuff that's out in the open. Include cabinets, cupboards, shelves, and closets on your feng shui housecleaning list. Stop sweeping that dust under the rug and get out the vacuum cleaner!

When you get in the habit of looking around your house with feng shui eyes, you will feel greater motivation to do the regular chores that go along with being a mindful caretaker of your home.

Yard at Work

Yard work is good feng shui, too. Real estate agents know this when they recommend cosmetic changes to improve the "curb appeal" of your house. If you've lived in your current home for more than a year, get in your car and drive around the neighborhood for a few minutes as if you were seeing it for the first time, then return to your block.

How does your home look compared to those of your neighbors? If you were in the market for a new home right now, would you be attracted to the one you live in? Why or why not? Are any of these reasons due to cosmetic problems that could be corrected with minimal effort and expense?

Small things like hedges that could use a trim, a brown patch in the lawn, or a swing set that's become rusty and neglected, can get a little worse day after day without attracting much attention. It's important to take a fresh look at your property at least once a year or with every change of seasons. Check the exterior of the house, too. Lilting shutters, peeling paint, and sagging gutters are signs of deteriorating chi, signaling that your home needs feng shui attention in the form of basic maintenance work.

 Feng Fact

Home improvements such as replacing old shutters, building a deck, or hiring a landscape designer to redo the yard are also good feng shui because they create a more attractive and comfortable environment. It's no surprise that this kind of good feng shui increases the resale value of your home.

Good feng shui requires a clean and well-maintained home and yard, but that doesn't mean you have to do all the work yourself. If you just don't have the time or really hate to do chores yourself, hire a maid and a lawn service to do the "rubber glove" feng shui for you. Can't afford domestic help? Use the feng shui techniques in this book to help increase your prosperity, and you may soon be able to afford that maid and lawn service you've been wanting for so long.

The Least You Need to Know

- Clean chi is good chi.
- Be sure to include cleaning out your cabinets, drawers, and closets in your feng shui strategy.
- First impressions are important: Make sure the outside of your house gets some feng shui attention, too.

Feng Shui Cures and How to Use Them

Here are descriptions of some objects and other "cures" that are commonly used in feng shui. Keep in mind as you choose what to place where in your home, that confidence in your cures is a very important ingredient in your success. If you do not find a particular object attractive, it does not belong in your home, regardless of how well a similar item may have worked for a friend; each time you see it, the feeling that you do not like it will counteract any positive effect it may be having.

Do not feel that you are limited to traditional feng shui objects or to the items listed in this section. Virtually anything can be used for a feng shui purpose once you understand the element cycles and match your item to the appropriate area of the ba gua (please refer to Chapter 3 for details). Trust your intuition, and if your gut says "don't use that," choose something else instead.

Suggested resources for where to shop for these and other feng shui items are provided in Appendix B.

Bamboo Flutes

Chinese bamboo flutes are used to lift oppressive energy such as that created by an exposed beam over your bed, desk, sofa, or dining table. Hang bamboo flutes in pairs with the top ends closer together, to mimic the angles of the top part of an octagon. If you can tell the growth direction of the bamboo (the oldest part will be wider, with the growth sections closer together), hang each flute with the root end at the bottom. Usually this will be with the mouthpiece at the top. If the growth direction is not obvious, hang each flute with the mouthpiece at the bottom to imply air moving upward through the flute. Traditionally, two red tassels dangle from each flute for additional positive energy.

Chinese Coins

Chinese coins are round with a small square hole in the center. This combination of shapes represents the union of heaven and earth and is a strong symbol of prosperity and good fortune. Most often these coins are used in multiples tied with red string or ribbon. Chinese coins are a good addition to your wealth area, kitchen, or near the front door to your home.

Color

Color is a very important aspect of feng shui. Each of the five elements and each area of the ba gua has one or more colors associated with it (see Chapter 3 for details). Here are some general color meanings to keep in mind as you choose accessories and décor for your home:

- Red: good fortune, energy, strength, success
- Yellow: health, happiness
- Brown: stability, contemplation
- Pink: romance
- White: purity
- Metallic colors: money
- Black: wisdom, mystery
- Blue: intuition, emotions, tranquility, spirituality
- Green: prosperity, growth, health
- Purple: wealth and success

Faceted Crystal Balls

Faceted crystal balls are a powerful feng shui cure for dispersing sha chi and creating a more balanced energy in a room. Use them anywhere you need to slow down fast-moving chi (such as in a long hallway) or to protect against sha chi from an overhead fixture such as a skylight, beam, or ceiling fan. They can also be used as enhancements to improve and activate the energy in a specific area. For example, a faceted crystal ball hung in the Marriage area of your bedroom can help to attract and encourage romance. In a window, a faceted crystal ball keeps chi from leaking out of the home and fills the room with colorful splashes of prismatic color.

Faceted crystal balls are a manmade cure, and should not be confused with natural crystals such as quartz or amethyst. (For more about these, see "Natural Crystals and Gemstones" later in this appendix.) Purity and quality are very important for this cure, so do invest in the best ones available: Swarovski crystals from Austria are preferred by feng shui professionals. For best effect, hang your crystal ball with a length of red string cut to a multiple of nine inches. Large, high-quality faceted crystal balls are not inexpensive; do get the largest size that you can afford, at least 30 mm or larger. The small, 20-mm crystals are good to hang on your key chain or from the rearview mirror of your car, but are not large enough to have much impact for other applications.

Firecrackers

The explosive energy of firecrackers is thought to be a powerful cure anywhere you need protection. Look for Chinese fake "firecrackers" of molded plastic made to look like five giant firecrackers set in a row; set them on the door frame above the inside of your front door to protect your home from negative energy.

Fragrance

Scent can have a powerful affect on emotions and mental activity. Incense and any kind of aromatherapy are appropriately used in feng shui. The result achieved will depend on the fragrance you select.

For example: peppermint and eucalyptus are stimulating; orange is purifying; ylang ylang is sensuous; lavender is calming. Any scent that is pleasing to you is good feng shui. Bad smells of any kind are a sign of sha chi, and should be investigated and cleared immediately.

Imagery

The imagery with which you fill your home has a powerful subconscious effect on your thoughts and emotions. In feng shui, every object, photograph, figurine, or work of art carries a symbolic meaning, depending on what it depicts. Examining every image in key areas of your home for obvious or even hidden meanings is an important part of your feng shui strategy. Keep in mind that meaning is often very personal. A piece of artwork that a friend may not like could have very positive and inspiring meaning for you.

For example, water scenes are generally considered to be very positive (since moving water is associated with cash flow), but a painting of a sailing ship caught in a storm would not be good feng shui because it portrays a scene of struggle and potential disaster. However, that painting could have personal meaning for you that is not obvious to everyone else. Perhaps it was painted by your late grandfather, and was one of his favorite works, so to you it has a positive association with memories of sitting beside your grandpa on a summer day watching him paint. Perhaps it was not easy for him to pursue his love of painting, and to you this work symbolized his perseverance in following his creative dream. Or perhaps you purchased the painting just after weathering a particularly stormy period in your life, and to you it is a powerful reminder that no matter how rough things get, you know you'll reach safe harbor eventually.

The potential symbolic meaning of artwork and imagery is virtually unlimited. Your own good judgment should be the deciding factor in whether or not you keep a particular image in your home, and where you choose to display it.

Light

All kinds of lights are representative of the fire element and have an energizing effect on your space. Dark spaces have low chi, making the simple addition of more or brighter lights a very easy and effective feng shui cure. Candles can also be used to bring more fire energy into a space. A pair of pink candles set side-by-side in the Marriage area of your bedroom can light a romantic fire in your love life; for greater passion and intensity use red candles instead.

Lucky Bamboo

"Lucky bamboo" is actually a variety of dracaena that grows well with minimal light and attention. Usually sold in small bundles set in pebbles in porcelain pots, lucky bamboo is a fun addition to the Wealth area of your desk, office, or home. In a bathroom, it will help to absorb some of the excess water energy, and in the kitchen it will help to keep the stove's fire energy strong.

Mirrors

Mirrors are often called "the aspirin of feng shui" because they are useful in so many different situations. They can …

- Create the impression of more light in a dark space.
- Create the impression of greater space in a small room.
- Symbolically create space for expansion of ideas and opportunities.
- Increase safety by expanding your field of vision.
- Allow your eyes a greater range of focus, which helps to release tension.
- Magnify the energy of anything that they reflect.
- Bring a beautiful outdoor view into an interior space through its reflection.

While they are extremely powerful and useful, mirrors do require some care in selection and placement. Mirrors that are hung too low, so that a tall family member cannot see his or her full reflection, can lead to poor self-image or a lack of inspiration. Any negative chi—such as an unattractive exterior view or interior clutter—that is reflected in the mirror will energetically be doubled. Mirrors in the bedroom are also thought to be disruptive to a good night's sleep.

A ba gua mirror is a specific cure consisting of a small round mirror in an eight-sided frame decorated with a pattern of trigrams (sets of three solid and/or broken lines). This kind of mirror is used to deflect sha chi aimed at the exterior of your home, and is often hung above or beside the front door. You should not use a ba gua mirror indoors, as this is thought to cause bad luck. You may see octagonal mirrors for sale described as "ba gua" mirrors, but be aware that this is not correct. An octagonal mirror can be used inside the home for luck. It is the octagonal *frame* around a small *round* mirror, along with the trigram decorations, that defines a ba gua mirror to be used outside for protection.

Concave mirrors can also be used for protection, because the image that they reflect appears smaller and upside down, symbolically diminishing its influence. Convex mirrors enlarge whatever they are reflecting and can be useful for providing a larger field of vision.

Movement

Flags, banners, whirligigs, and mobiles of any kind can be used to activate dull, stagnant chi, to attract attention (and therefore, chi) to the front door or another important area of the home, or to lift the energy of a specific area of your yard. A gently moving mobile can also be used to soothe chaotic energy. Be sure that the color and/or imagery of your moving object matches or supports the area where you plan to use it.

Natural Crystals and Gemstones

Natural crystals carry powerful energy from the earth in which they are formed. Their energy is more complex than that of the manmade faceted crystal balls. Different kinds of natural crystals are thought to have different effects due to the differences in their structure and vibration. For example:

- Amethyst is considered a very spiritual crystal.
- Clear quartz brings clarity and balance.
- Turquoise is associated with prosperity.
- Citrine is thought to bring luck.
- Moonstone is associated with intuition.
- Rose quartz is good for romance.
- Black onyx helps in breaking through limitations.

These are just a few examples of the many varieties of natural stones and crystals that you can select to use as chi adjustments.

Plants and Flowers

Living plants of all kinds bring the energy of nature, growth, and vitality into your home. Flowers are a popular feng shui cure because in addition to their visual beauty they add color and fragrance to the plant's positive energy. Plants and flowers are appropriate for virtually any area of the home, and are especially recommended if you wish to strengthen fire or control water energy. It is acceptable to use artificial plants rather than live ones, so long as they are as realistic as possible in appearance. Silk flowers are fine; cheap plastic ones should be avoided. Dried flowers are not recommended for feng shui, because their vitality is completely depleted. That's not to say that you should remove all dried flowers from your home, as long as you only keep those that you truly cherish, and understand that they are not effective as feng shui cures. It's also a good idea to take a look at what area of the ba gua they are in, both in terms of your entire home and within that specific room. If you really love that heart-shaped wreath made from dried pink rosebuds, it's okay to keep it. But don't hang it in the Marriage area of your bedroom thinking it will help to attract a romantic partner.

Religious Figures and Imagery

Any kind of religious imagery that supports your spiritual beliefs and practice is appropriate for feng shui. If your décor includes religious imagery from a culture other than your own, be sure you know what that figure or symbol represents and that it is appropriate for the space in which you have placed it. The Knowledge area of the ba gua, also associated with spirituality, is a good place for religious imagery or a home altar.

Sound

Bells and wind chimes are very frequently used in feng shui where there is a need for some kind of alarm or protection, such as if your front door is directly in the path of sha chi. These cures can also be used inside the house, even where there is no air current to sound them. The symbolic power of the object is an effective cure even if it rarely makes a sound. Sound also enlivens a space, and music can be used to either stimulate or calm a space depending on how it affects your mood.

Texture

The texture of a fabric or other surface affects both how it looks and how it feels. The textures of your floor coverings, curtains, upholstery, and even walls and ceilings contribute to the mood of each room. For example, imagine how the cool tile of the bathroom floor feels against your bare feet compared to the soft carpeting in your bedroom. Soft textures like wall-to-wall carpeting and velvet or chenille upholstery make a room feel warmer, cozier, and friendlier, and invite you to sit down and relax. Compare those to the feelings evoked by smooth, hard surfaces such as marble tile, hardwood floors, and glass-topped tables.

If something feels not-quite-right about a space, consider whether textures may be part of the problem. Think about adding (or removing) an area rug, exchanging that sleek chrome and leather chair for an upholstered armchair, or replacing those heavy drapes with plantation shutters in order to change the feeling of the room. Keep in mind that one person's "cozy" is another person's "claustropho-bic," so only you can decide whether or not you are happy with the effects created by the materials and décor of your home.

Water Fountains

Moving water is associated with prosperity in feng shui, which accounts for the popularity of water fountains as feng shui cures. Best used beside the front door, or in the Wealth or Career area of the home, fountains are not recommended in the bed-room where they can be disruptive to your sleep. If a real fountain is not appropriate for some reason, use photographs or artwork of a river or waterfall instead.

As you choose your feng shui objects and place them in your home, pay attention to thoughts or feelings that may arise; they can reveal any inner resistance you might feel about actually achieving your goals. For example, perhaps you have selected a beautiful bowl to place in your Wealth area, and have filled it with fruit or uncooked rice to symbol-ize abundance. Looking at your arrangement, you become aware of the feeling that "this will never work for me." Thoughts like these are clear signs of unresolved issues that may have to do with low self-worth, a pessimistic outlook, or a lack of confi-dence in your ability to experience a better life.

These inner beliefs have a powerful energy of their own that can interfere with the workings of your feng shui changes. If thoughts or issues such as these arise for you, pay attention to them, and make a commitment to doing the inner work that will help to support your outer transformations.

Appendix B

Resources

Books and eBooks

There are literally thousands of feng shui books on the market, with more being published every day. Here is a list of some of my favorites.

Contemporary Western Feng Shui

Chin, R.D. *Feng Shui Revealed: An Aesthetic, Practical Approach to the Ancient Art of Space Alignment.* Clarkson N. Potter, 1998.

Collins, Terah Kathryn. *The Western Guide to Feng Shui: Creating Balance, Harmony and Prosperity in Your Environment.* Hay House, 1996.

Linn, Denise. *Feng Shui for the Soul.* Hay House, 2000.

Roberts, Stephanie. *Fast Feng Shui: 9 Simple Principles for Transforming Your Life by Energizing Your Home.* Lotus Pond Press, 2001.

————. *Fast Feng Shui for Prosperity: 8 Steps on the Path to Abundance.* Lotus Pond Press, 2004.

————. *Fast Feng Shui for Singles: 108 Ways to Heal Your Home and Attract Romance.* Lotus Pond Press, 2002.

Thompson, Angel. *Feng Shui: How to Achieve the Most Harmonious Arrangement of Your Home and Office.* St. Martin's Griffin, 1996.

Traditional Chinese Feng Shui

Moran, Elizabeth, Master Joseph Yu, and Master Val Biktashev. *The Complete Idiot's Guide to Feng Shui.* Alpha Books, 2002.

Too, Lillian. *The Illustrated Encyclopedia of Feng Shui.* Element Books, 2000.

Wong, Eva. *Feng Shui: The Ancient Wisdom of Harmonious Living for Modern Times.* Shambhala, 1996.

Related Topics

Kingston, Karen. *Creating Sacred Space with Feng Shui.* Broadway, 1997.

Leeds, Regina. *Sharing a Place Without Losing Your Space: A Couple's Guide to Blending Homes, Lives, and Clutter.* Alpha Books, 2003.

————. *The Zen of Organizing: Creating Order and Peace in Your Home, Career, and Life.* Alpha Books, 2002.

Marcus, Clare Cooper. *House as a Mirror of Self: Exploring the Deeper Meaning of Home.* Conari Press, 1995.

Mendelson, Cheryl. *Home Comforts: The Art and Science of Keeping House.* Scribner, 1999.

Roberts, Stephanie. *Clutter-Free Forever! Home Coaching Program.* Lotus Pond Press, 2003.

Robyn, Kathryn L. *Spiritual Housecleaning: Healing the Space Within by Beautifying the Space Around You.* New Harbinger, 2001.

Silley, Marla. *Sink Reflections.* Bantam, 2002.

Websites

Here is a short list of helpful Internet sources for feng shui information and products. You can also find feng shui products at many New Age retailers. When shopping for feng shui products at general purpose sites/stores, be aware that these retailers often know little or nothing about feng shui except that it sells, and you may find that a "feng shui" label is given to anything of vaguely Asian origin. Do not take a "feng shui" item name as proof that it is a traditional (or even useful) product. Always be guided by your own taste and style. If you like something, you can probably find a good feng shui use for it based on color, material, or the theme (wealth, marriage, etc.) that it represents to you.

www.astro-fengshui.com. Traditional Chinese feng shui information and training from Master Joseph Yu.

www.clutterfreeforever.com. Clutter-clearing advice from a feng shui perspective.

www.dragon-gate.com. Extensive feng shui supplies and useful information to help you choose and use Chinese feng shui objects.

www.ebay.com. Do a search for "feng shui" and a wide variety of items will come up. Good values on useful items are usually available if you are prepared to wade through some junk.

www.fastfengshui.com. The author's website, including newsletter archives, FAQs, articles, tips, books, and frequently updated links to a wide range of related sites, including our approved vendors for wind chimes, water fountains, and other feng shui products.

www.fengshuiebooks.com. Fast Feng Shui ebooks and free ebooklets for instant download.

www.fengshuiemporium.com. Books, products, and information in all areas of feng shui, including a practitioner directory.

www.fengshuiguild.com. The website of the International Feng Shui Guild, including articles and a practitioner directory.

www.inmcrystal.com. Excellent prices, value, and selection. This is where I shop for crystals. From the home page, click on "crystal prisms" and then select item #3550 for the faceted crystal balls used in feng shui.

www.pacificspiritcatalogs.com. New Age gift catalog with some feng shui items. Please note that the item they sell as a "ba gua mirror" is not a ba gua mirror. The item they sell as a "feng shui mirror" is a ba gua mirror and is appropriate for use as a feng shui cure as described in this book.

www.pyramidcollection.com. A general gift catalog with some items appropriate for use as feng shui accessories.

Index